Love Never Dies:

Embracing Grief with Hope & Promise

Larry M. Barber, LPC-S, CT

xulon
PRESS

This book is dedicated to my one true friend who has been with me always providing the support, comfort, encouragement, grace, mercy, unconditional love and hope that I have needed.

Each page is a tribute to every one of His friends, family members and messengers who have acted for my benefit and the benefit of my two greatest joys in this life, my son Christian and my daughter Sarah.

"Christ gives me the strength to face anything."
Philippians 4:13 CEV

TABLE OF CONTENTS

FOREWORD

"**D**o you know Larry Barber?" I was asked.
"I know *about* him. I heard him speak at church several years ago about his grief journey after the death of his wife and daughter. But I don't know him personally," I said.

"He might be the one who could fill this position," she told me.

In January of 2007 ChristianWorks for Children was faced with the task of rebuilding a counseling ministry and restoring a children and teen grief support ministry. As the Executive Director and CEO it was my responsibility to accomplish the task. During a thirty-five year business career I had built and developed several organizations in marketing, manufacturing, and finance. I knew little about counseling and less about grief support for kids. We began to search for Larry Barber.

My prior experience had taught me to begin rebuilding by writing the Personal Profile for the ideal person to lead these ministries and excel in the position. Then I could hope for finding someone who could fill seventy percent of the ideal requirements.

My experience as a Christian taught me to begin to pray for God to provide the person for His ministry and that I would recognize the person when presented.

I did not know that God had put in motion a series of events after a tragic happening that would give Larry Barber an unparalleled opportunity to fulfill a promise he had made to Him in July of 1993.

The ideal Personal Profile read:

- o Education: Advanced Degree in Counseling, Degree in Bible or Ministry.
- o Experience: Professional knowledge and practice in cognitive therapy for all ages.
- o Facilitates support groups for emotional and mental disorders.
- o Life experience processing his or her personal grief preferably as a parent.
- o Relationship to God: An Everyday Christian knowing prayer and scripture are relevant to life issues today.
- o Credentials: Licensed Professional Counselor, Licensed Supervisor Preferred.

Larry Barber, with Certification in Thanatology, exceeded the Personal Profile. Of course, God had uniquely prepared him for this role at this time and I'm thankful He let me see it. Larry provides uniquely keen insight for mourners and those that comfort and care for the bereaved through the revelation of his personal grief journey as a husband and father, and through the journey of his children. Combined with his preparation and experience as a Licensed Professional Counselor, as a minister with a Master's Degree in Biblical Studies, and the promise he made to God — his insight into grief and mourning is life changing for the mourner and the caregiver.

Love Never Dies encourages the mourner to embrace grief as a natural expression of love for a person that died. Grief resides in the community of 1 Corinthians 13:7 where love is described as the emotion that "bears all things, believes all things, hopes all things, endures all things." This is an important book for all mourners, and their counselors, therapists, ministers, pastors, chaplains and friends to allow the grief experience to be a healing one and not a fearful one.

Larry pilots the mourner and care giver through understanding the dichotomy of grief. While it is universal and natural in what it expresses, it is unique in how it is experienced by each individual. The mourner is liberated from the societal requirements of compliance with a standard process and set time frame in which to "deal with it and move on." Care givers will find relief from thinking they must be the advisor or director of the mourner's grief. They will see that coming alongside and walking with a mourner during this dark time is significantly more valuable to the mourner.

Larry Barber was hired by ChristianWorks for Children in April of 2007 as Director of GriefWorks and CounselingWorks ministries. In his work thousands of all ages have received comfort and care in navigating their own grief journey. He is the one that God had prepared to fill this position to honor a promise made in prayer.

Robert E. Pine
Executive Director, ChristianWorks for Children
President, Enterprise Christian Ministry
Trustee, Christian Care Centers
February 2011

INTRODUCTION

A GRIEF UNPREPARED

Wednesday, April 6, 1967. The den of my family's house.

"Larry, I have something sad to tell you," said my father entering the room. He had just returned from an evening church service. My mother and I had stayed at home because we were ill. "Larry, I don't know how to tell you this... but your friend Stanley Johnson drowned this afternoon."

No one had prepared me for all the death and loss that I would inevitably experience in my life. I wish now that someone had.

In 1967 one of my closest friends Stanley Johnson drowned at Lake Pat Cleburne. Stanley was running laps around the lake with his high school teammates when someone got the great idea that they could take a short cut swim across the lake and cool off in the process. Stanley never made it out of the water. No one had prepared me for the emotional chaos and pain that would result from the death of a best friend who had lived less than seventeen years. I didn't know that Death could take young, talented, full of life people such as Stanley. Suddenly the world had become a very unsafe, unfair place.

No one taught me about the true nature of grief, its purpose and the struggle it brings into a life. I grew up a child of the sixties. All of my generation looked to the models of grief that were held up by the culture. We had all admired the classy, stoicism of First Lady Jackie Kennedy with her emotionless face behind a black veil at her husband's funeral. We told ourselves, "Now she is handling grief well. She is being strong for her children and the nation." After Stanley's death I felt anything but strong or stoic.

I wish someone had prepared me for saying good bye to someone that I loved. At Stanley's funeral it was my first experience at understanding how awful the pain of loss could be. The first dead body I saw was my dear classmate and friend. No one had told me about open casket services. No one had explained to me that we would all file past the casket only feet away from a corpse. At age sixteen I experienced overwhelming horror and panic because no one had explained the routine rituals of a funeral.

I wish someone had prepared me for all the feelings that would flood over me as I was confronted that warm spring day by the realities of my loss. After the funeral, I sobbed and wailed uncontrollably in the back seat of our family car. I was inconsolable. How could I and Life go on without a valuable person and friend such as Stanley?

My parents suggested that maybe it was best for me not to go to the graveside ceremony. The unintentional message that my loving parents sent me was that I was not handling the loss well. "Maybe we should just go home now, Larry, and think about something else," my mother said.

From that moment it seemed as if everyone was advising me that I needed to forget loved ones who die and move on. To this day I have never been able to forget Stanley, the memories of our friendship and how he influenced my life. I don't want to forget. I don't want to leave my dear friend in the past. I wish someone had told me then that remembering Stanley and crying was not unhealthy or pathological.

What I thought I knew about death and grief, what I had learned from watching other mourners, and what I did not know then about the true nature of grief have shaped how I have mourned for decades. My misconceptions and lack of knowledge have complicated my grief for my friend Stanley, my family members and others I have lost to Death. My misconceptions and lack of knowledge about death and grief have in many ways complicated my life, my relationships and my spiritual walk.

Grief can never be easy, but understanding the real nature of grief and the causes of our pain can make the struggle easier. Learning to live without a precious loved one or friend in your life is always difficult. Because our culture does not prepare us for death and loss, the process of grief becomes even more complicated. Knowledge about dying, death and grief can prepare us to make wiser, healthier choices during the darkest times of life. *The real experts of grief, the experienced mourners all around us, can provide us with that knowledge. All we have to do to prepare for our grief journey is to be open and listen to them.*

There is no cookie cutter guide or one set of rules for every grief. We mourners must find our own personal path through loss. How we mourn must fit our unique individual situation and needs. This book outlines how I have processed my own losses and grief experience. It is not a prescription for all grief. It is a description of my observations in dealing with my own losses and what others have taught me about their journeys toward good, healthy mourning. <u>I am an expert only on my grief. You are the expert on your own grief.</u> Take from this book what works for you and use it.

My hope for you is that you equip yourself with knowledge about the true nature of grief and how it applies to you and your loss. I want you to have the hope that you will receive exactly what you need to move through grief toward healing from the emotional trauma of loss. I want you to know the joy and peace of good mourning and a good life.

Congratulations on the courage you are showing daily in facing your grief and searching for the help, support and comfort you need. I believe that no one was meant to go through grief alone and without hope. My expectation is that this book and the personal experiences and insights of other mourners can help you with your passage through grief.

Brothers and sisters, we do not want you to be uninformed about those who sleep in death, so that you do not grieve like the rest of mankind, who have no hope. …… <u>encourage one another with these words.</u> (I Thessalonians 4:13, 18 NIV)

CHAPTER ONE

TWO PRAYERS
AND A PROMISE

Thursday, July 15, 1993: In the waiting room outside a counseling office

Everybody knew what I needed. At least that's how it seemed. Two months after the deaths of my 37 year old wife Cindy and my two year old adopted daughter Katie in a multi-car accident, everybody had advice for me—friends, family, co-workers, church members and well-meaning acquaintances. Everybody knew how to live my life, handle my grief, and parent my two grieving children. Everybody knew except me.

I couldn't decide exactly what I needed. In the first days and weeks after the accident I felt like I was drowning in groups of fawning folks who were there to help me. So I wanted everyone to go away and just give me space to breathe and think.

In just weeks after the accident and the double funeral service, I got my wish of being alone. All my comforters disappeared. They returned to their jobs, families and lives just as they had been before the accident. It seemed to me so unfair that they could return to everything as normal for them and as if the deaths had never occurred. I felt lonely and angry as the emotional numbness of my initial grief wore off and the pains of my new life became real.

I did know one thing. I wanted the suffering and emotional pain which had become my new world and the new reality for my son and daughter to end…or at least decrease to a manageable level. I vacillated between two conditions: being completely numb, lethargic, apathetic and empty or being overwhelmed by a combination of painful emotions and thoughts which I had never experienced.

I also knew that after sixty days of trying everything I had used previously to cope with life crises, my life and emotional state seemed to be worsening. A deep dark despair was growing inside me. My grief was a spiritual black hole that threatened to swallow me and everything I had valued. It was obvious even to me that I was powerless on my own. So I accepted the generous offer of help from my boss to pay for my trip to a grief counselor.

As I sat down in the counselor's waiting room with a clipboard of paperwork to complete, I began to have second thoughts. "Why did you come here? The counselor is going to make you talk about everything and that will make you sad and hurt even more. What good will talking about losing Cindy and Katie do? It won't bring them back and that's the only way to fix things. This is a waste of time. Save yourself further torture. Get up and leave now!"

I really don't know why I stayed seated and, without revisiting my doubts, began to fill in the blanks on the counseling forms. But I did. It was surprisingly easy. Name, address and phone number. Okay, I could do these without thinking and without hurting. That is until I came to "Marital Status."

Without warning I was forced into making another painful choice. I couldn't mark married, or could I? I really didn't feel single so I couldn't check that box. I wasn't divorced. Then there was "WIDOWED." The word burned into my consciousness with a new and awful realization. Not only had I been robbed of my wife and daughter, but I had my identity stolen and replaced with a new identity that no one would choose.

"WIDOWED." No longer would others see me as a husband, as part of a loving, happy couple or the head of a complete, happy household. "WIDOWED." How I hated that word and the new identity that had been stamped across my forehead.

No longer would I be known as Larry Barber, husband and father. Whenever anyone saw me now they would say to others, "Oh, yeah. That's Larry Barber. Poor man. It's so sad. He's the one who lost his wife and daughter in a horrible accident. He's *WIDOWED*."

The new reality struck me with the same force that I had felt that horrific moment on Saturday May 15, 1993 minutes after the "other driver" struck the car carrying my entire family of five almost head-on. Sitting in the wreckage of our car I had been awakened by hearing someone's prayer:

Dear Jesus, be with me and my family. Please, Jesus, be with us. Please be with us.

As I stared out into a broken car windshield and my eyes wandered over the chaos of twisted metal surrounding me, the praying continued:

Please, Jesus, be with us. Please be with us. Be with all of us.

The driver's seat where my wife had been sitting was gone. In fact the whole driver's side was a gaping, jagged hole. I was unaware that my wife Cindy had been thrown from the car and was now lying on the pavement with emergency medical technicians surrounding her. They were already assessing her multiple external and internal wounds that would end up taking her life just two days later.

I heard my twelve year old son Christian's worried cry "My eye. Oh, my eye!" I turned to look into the back seat of our small Ford Escort. Christian and my nine year old daughter Sarah were both gone. I could not see that Christian was hanging halfway out of the hatchback door which had popped open on impact. Unfortunately my searching eyes then watched as an EMT lifted my two year old daughter Katie lifeless and still buckled in her child safety seat. Katie had been sitting behind the driver's seat where her mother had been only minutes before the crash. Katie died instantly.

Someone's prayer continued, *Please, Jesus, be with us. Oh, please be with us.* I suddenly realized that the someone praying was me.

I sat with my physical and emotional trauma enveloping me in a darkness that I had never experienced. I was paralyzed by the fear that I could lose everything that was precious to me in this life. I prayed for help for my family and a feeling of Jesus' comforting presence. The prayer echoed up from the depths of my frantic soul.

In my own personal hell of the moment, I felt all alone and helpless. Only now years later I realize that the prayer was answered. My daughter Sarah had been thrown from the vehicle. Among her injuries was a broken femur which would cause her to endure surgery, weeks of traction and more weeks in a lower body cast and wheelchair.

We may not always feel God's presence in trauma. In my pain and turmoil I could not feel Him at all moments after the accident on an Arlington, Texas interstate highway. But God heard my prayer, provided His Son's presence and spared me and my family further trauma. Sarah was found minutes after the accident by a former police officer turned car salesman who witnessed the accident from a nearby auto dealership. The former police officer administered CPR to her limp body. Her heart and her breathing had stopped when she was thrown from the car.

EMT's told me later that Sarah would have most likely died if it had not been for the man trained in CPR being on the scene soon after the crash. I know that God answered my prayer that day and that He continues to be with me and my family today.

Now outside a counselor's office seeking help two months after the accident, the painful emotional impact of the loss of my identity and purpose sent my soul again into a prayer rising from my helplessness and need for rescue:

Lord, please send me help. Send someone to help me. Send anyone. Send people and information into my life that can help us. Tell me how my children and I can get through this.

And Lord, if you will just send that message, support and comfort to help, I will gladly share that message with others who need it in their lives.

Here is an important thought to remember. You should make promises judiciously, especially promises to God. He has the ability to make all things possible for you to keep your word. For me this promise made to God was no mistake and continues to be a source of healing and blessings for me.

As a grief facilitator I have been able to learn healing insights from hundreds of grief experts. I have also been given countless opportunities to share as a fellow mourner and as a bereavement counselor with hurting people the knowledge and insights that have been shared with me about death, dying and grief.

My call for rescue has been answered in part through my classroom education in the pursuit of two Masters Degrees to become a minister and a licensed professional counselor. God has blessed me with knowledge about life and loss through highly qualified instructors. But noted, trained bereavement experts are not my only teachers.

I have heard from other special grief messengers who have been taught by their life experiences. These messengers sent in answer to my prayer include mourning children, teens and adults who have taught me lessons that have changed the way I see death, dying and bereavement. My trainers in grief have taught me through my work as a counselor, a hospice bereavement coordinator and as Director of GriefWorks, a children's grief support ministry in Dallas, Texas.

My most valued grief messengers have been clients and fellow mourners who taught me that grief does not always have to stay overwhelming and all consuming. The grief experience and mourners can change. There is hope to be found even in the darkest times of life.

Grief will never be easy, but the burdens of loss can be lightened with the support of others, their experience and their knowledge. The grief-changing insights shared can give mourners no matter what their background, culture or beliefs the perspectives of grief necessary to maintain hope that there will be a time for their own personal rescue, joy, healing and peace of mind.

It is my hope that this book gives me further opportunities to share with you and other fellow mourners, caregivers and bereavement professionals the insights that can lighten the load of grief. I hope these insights and experiences shared can change how you and others perceive and deal with grief. Unfortunately many mourners and their professional caregivers see grief as something to be avoided, gotten over, cured or eliminated.

I hope the insights will also stop caregivers and professionals from seeing grief as an illness from which to be recovered, a disorder to be diagnosed and treated, or a condition that needs to be resolved or fixed. The message I have received from grief experts is that mourners are not sick and that they are not broken. Mourners are experiencing the natural human response to the death of someone they love or with whom they have a special emotional relationship.

Meanwhile as my grief training continues, I persist in prayer asking to learn from the experts of grief and to be faithful to my promise to share with other mourners. My hope for you is that you be blessed in your grief with messages and messengers that allow you to experience comfort, support and a reason to hope for what lies ahead.

"I've thrown myself headlong into your arms— I'm celebrating your rescue. I'm singing at the top of my lungs,

I'm so full of answered prayers." (Psalms 13:4-6 The Message)

NOTE TO READER: What if I have a different background or beliefs than those of the author or other mourners cited in this book?

Mourners do not need to share the belief system or grief experience of the author or those whose stories illustrate the grief insights in this book in order to benefit from these insights. The new perspectives discussed in this book are common threads that run through many different grief experiences.

All mourners of all beliefs have the potential for learning and grieving in a healthy way, to heal, to enjoy life and to maintain hope for the future. I ask you to keep an open mind and heart for what the grief experts sent into your life have to share with you. Use what is beneficial and meaningful to you in your personal grief journey. Share what is beneficial and meaningful with other mourners you encounter in their individual grief journeys.

In the years that I have been involved in facilitating grief support groups, in directing grief seminars and in individual grief counseling, I have intentionally fostered a "belief-friendly" healing environment. Mourners, their individual situations and their expressed feelings and beliefs need to be heard without judgment or unsolicited advice.

Although mourners share some experiences and emotions in common, there are no two griefs exactly alike. Each mourner is "the" expert on his or her unique grief. Each mourner has the power to choose his or her path through grief.

In a belief-friendly atmosphere, all mourners are accepted where they are and "companioned" in their distinct individual grief experience. (Read the works of Alan D. Wolfelt, Ph.D. on the Companioning Model versus the Medical Model of Bereavement Support. Dr. Wolfelt is the director of the Center for Loss and Life Transition in Fort Collins, Colorado.)

Judgment by you or others of the mourner's beliefs, feelings and experiences is not allowed in a belief-friendly atmosphere. Each mourner honors and accepts the thoughts and feelings of others' grief experiences. In a belief-friendly environment each mourner learns from the other in the healing process despite differences in life situations, beliefs and opinions.

It is my hope that you can maintain a belief-friendly attitude as you read the grief insights in this book. Use what will work for you, your beliefs and your circumstances to mourn in a healthy manner.

CHAPTER TWO

LOVE NEVER DIES: THE NATURE OF GRIEF

Grief is never easy, but it is often as complex and over-whelming as the mourner perceives it to be. *In our culture many mourners view grief as an odious, inevitable reality which is to be dreaded, feared, contained or avoided. No wonder countless grievers suffer with what others label as complicated, prolonged or pathological grief. When grief is seen for what it is ....the burden of grief can be lightened.*

The waiting room outside my counseling office.

In today's session Ken sat on the couch across from me, smiled and exclaimed, "I stopped it! The uncontrollable crying. I stopped it!"

In Ken's first counseling session the week prior I had been at a loss as the 59 year old self-avowed "Momma's boy" cried and expressed an overpowering despair. He had been completely inconsolable over the death of his 82 year old mother.

As a fledgling bereavement counselor new to hospice, I had walked away from his initial session wondering if I could ever be able to help Ken. I even wondered if I was cut out for this sort of work. His inability to see any reason for joy and hope had silenced me for almost the entire hour. I had no answers or wise words for Ken that could take away his pain. In this second session, I had braced myself for more tears and utter hopelessness.

For all of Ken's life prior to his mother's death, each had been all the other had. Ken's birth father had abandoned them when Ken was an infant. Therefore, Ken and his mother Evelyn shared a "you and me against the world" relationship. Each had been the other's close friend, confidante, cheerleader, and life coach.

A successful businessman, Ken had never married and neither had his mother. Failing health had forced her to move in with her son, and he had been her primary caregiver for the last five years before her death from Parkinson's Disease. Ken's despondency and emotional desolation had been unlike many of the other hospice family members I had counseled. Most mourning adult children I had seen were sad but accepting of their elderly parent's death. Ken had expected to always have his mother there when he needed her and could not reconcile his new life without her.

In the first session Ken had expressed absolute despair and anger that every time he thought he was making progress in his grief, the memories of his mother would intrude. With those memories came a bleak sadness that caused him to surrender to sadness and "cry like a baby."

I tried reminding Ken that he was still early in his grief and that crying uncontrollably is natural and healthy. Ken would have none of that. He had replied, "It might be natural, but I can't keep doing this. I feel like once I let the crying start that it will never stop! I get so mad while crying that I yell for mother to leave me alone and stop making me so miserable."

In today's session Ken was a different man. Instead of an aura of despair, a sense of joy surrounded him. He excitedly shared with me that after several unpleasant crying spells, he had come to a surprising conclusion. "I always enjoyed visiting with mother *because I love her,*" he explained. "*And because I still love her,* the memories of her remind me how much I want to be with her again."

With tears streaming down his face Ken said that he realized his grief caused by his love for his mother was now the only connection that he still had with her. "*The tears…the grief are my love for my mother,*" he beamed. "So now when the memories and gloom come, I say, 'Hello, Mother. It's good to see you again.' And then we have a good visit."

Ken was ecstatic and I was stunned. This, of course, was a turning point in his early grief. Ken's insight that grief is love was a monumental jump for him toward healing from the emotional trauma of loss. The realization did not stop Ken from mourning and missing his mother. The new insight powerfully changed how he viewed his grief, how he processed it and how he expressed it. He saw his grief outbursts as positive, healthy events and not as something to be feared and avoided.

Most importantly, knowing that his grief was a connection to his mother produced by his love caused Ken's grief to be changed in two significant ways. First, the realization stopped Ken's struggle against experiencing his grief in a meaningful and therapeutic way. Now he could embrace his mother's once intrusive visits into his thoughts. Second, Ken maintained his love for his mother and their relationship despite her death. Although Ken had lost the physical presence of his mother in the relationship, he was still connected to her emotionally and spiritually.

Ken's insight that grief is love and that relationships do not end with death was also an eye opening moment for me as a bereavement specialist. I had learned that grief is simply another expression of the love or emotional investment that the mourner has for the one who has died. Grief is not just the result of love and loss. Grief is a continuation of the love for the person who died combined with the mourner's yearning to be in the loved one's presence just one more time.

<u>Now I was armed as a grief counselor and group facilitator with a concept that could reframe how all my clients see their grief and their relationship with their loved one</u>. The concept confirmed my belief and that of other bereavement specialists who accept the grief theories of continuing bonds. In these theories mourners do not detach from their loved one but work at maintaining healthy emotional attachments to the person who died.

Death does not kill relationships. However Death does change relationships. The change is that Death removes the physical presence of our loved one from the relationship bond, but the spiritual and emotional attachments to the loved one remain and can be nurtured.

The real struggle of grief comes from a natural human response to protest in any way possible the new reality of life without the physical presence of the person who died. The thought that one moment a loved one is there and the next minute gone is a harsh, painful concept to wrap the mind around. Mourners know and understand the facts of death and loss, but they do not want to feel forced to accept and live with this distressing new reality.

Let me preface what I am about to say by letting you know that I do not consider mourners childish or immature. I am not belittling your feelings or behavior. However in grief we mourners can be like the toddler throwing a tantrum. The toddler resorts to vigorous protest because he or she is helpless otherwise to change the situation that he or she does not like or want.

Death and "giving up" our loved one is not our wish and this is not the way that we feel life should be. Therefore, we as protesting mourners can create a longer, harder struggle for ourselves in grief. We do not wish to stop loving the one who has died, and we do not wish to leave the person in our past. So we rail against reality <u>and</u> moving toward healing.

<u>Knowing that grief is love expressed for the person who died helps us as mourners understand that we do not have to "give up", "let go", or "detach" from the one who died.</u> As mourners we can realize that we are not forced to forget or leave the person in our past. We live with the comforting thought that we can carry loved ones into our future. Knowing grief is love is an empowering insight which does not eliminate totally the struggle of grief, but it can make the intense, fierce battle against the loss and its consequences shorter in duration and less difficult.

Knowing that grief is love can influence the mourner's grief path, well being, and the quality of his or her life. This change of perspective on the true nature of grief after the death can cause mourners to approach grief in new ways resulting in less emotional struggles and complications:

- **The grief experience is reframed as a part of life with a positive purpose to be accepted and embraced rather than avoided.**
Usually mourners want to avoid grief because it is painful and seems like a waste of time. They think, "Why grieve if it doesn't change anything?" and "Why hurt when I can just try to forget and to find joy in life again?" When mourners realize their grief feelings are their love for the person, they choose to continue the love expressed as grief. Mourners can view their grief as natural and a part of healing.

- **Remembering the loved one can be more of a comforting occurrence rather than a painful event.**
Just as Ken realized his grief was the loving connection he still had with his mother, you and other mourners can learn to see memories and the resulting grief outbursts you experience as positive events. Time spent in grief becomes valued time spent visiting and honoring a loved one.

    Remembering the love one and mourning can be a source of joy, comfort and accomplishment for the mourner. As one bereaved parent dealing with the loss of her eight year old daughter killed in a traffic accident said, "I am looking forward to the day that when I think and talk about my daughter, I smile or laugh instead of cry."

- **Grief can act as a transition from life with the loved one physically present to life still**

31

connected to the loved one emotionally and spiritually.
Mourners moving from life with their loved one into life without their loved one present need some sort of psychological and spiritual transition. Grief becomes that loving, supporting transition to help ease the mourner into this new reality that no one wants to willingly accept. Grief has many purposes, and one of them is preparing us for living without the physical company of our loved one.

- **Mourners feel empowered to carry their loved one into the future with them rather than forced to forget and leave him or her in the past.**
Mourners have two great fears. The first fear is that their loved one will be forgotten. The second fear is that *they* will forget the loved one. Many times these fears keep the mourner from taking steps to progress in grief because they feel it means "giving up" or abandoning a loved one. It is not unusual for a mourner to feel extreme guilt whenever they experience joy, happiness or any positive emotion after the death. Knowing that grief is love expressed after a death gives them permission to feel joy and to proceed in grief.

- **Mourners realize by embracing grief despite its pain and discomfort that they are living healthy lives in honor of the loved one.**
Often I invite clients to do a mental exercise. I ask them to imagine that <u>they</u> are the ones who have died. What would they want for their loved ones left behind? Mourners usually say things

such as happiness, joy, peace, contentment and a meaningful life. Then I tell them, "That's what your loved one wants for you." The best memorial you can ever build to honor your loved one and his or her wishes for you would be to grieve in a healthy way and live a good life.

When mourners follow the conventional and historical wisdom of counselors all the way back to Freud that they must "let go" or "detach" (*decathexis* is the term used) from the object of their love or emotional investment, grief becomes an unwanted, painful, complicated reality and burden. The admonition that the only healthy way to progress in grief is to "let go" or "detach" from the one who died has caused many mourners to choose one of two unhealthy responses to loss.

The first common unhealthy grief response results from rebelling against "giving up" or forgetting about their loved one in order to heal. Mourners taking this grief path hold on to their loved one by clinging to the past and a relationship that cannot exist in the same form as it did prior to the death.

As a result these mourners use all their energies to keep the past alive. In fact, they expend more energy to stubbornly hang on to history than the energy it would take to acknowledge and adapt to the new reality. They are unable to maintain a loving, healthy relationship that can now be experienced emotionally and spiritually, but not physically. Their endless yearning for the reality that can no longer exist robs them of the healing and joy they could experience now. They think erroneously that healthy grieving makes it impossible to carry their loved one and their memories into the future with them.

The second common unhealthy grief response is for the mourner to run from or eliminate any memory of the loved one and the death. Mourners taking this grief path spend the majority of their time and energy in avoidance or denial of their grief and its emotions. The yearning they have for getting over grief, moving on and stopping the pain causes them to stifle the healthy expression of emotions and thoughts. The acknowledgement of these thoughts and emotions could move the mourner toward healing. Instead these mourners fail to maintain any relationship with the loved one—healthy or unhealthy—and they usually experience constant sadness, despair and misery. They are unable to fully experience the joy that is possible for them in their new reality.

The majority of grief clients that I have counseled have convinced me that "letting go" of a loved one is not an option for them. Their loved ones are a part of who they are and will be. Many times mourners express the feeling that they always carry their loved one inside them wherever they go. In a very real way mourners do take what their loved one has given them and pass it on to others. Knowing that grief is love gives the mourner a superior option to grief. The better option for mourners can be to choose to maintain their love for the person in a new healthy, healing relationship.

Since grief is the continued expression of love, to stop grieving over a person is to stop loving him or her. As one widow in a grief support group asked me, "You mean I don't have to leave my husband in the past? Are you saying that I can take him into the future with me?" The answer is a resounding, comforting and hope-filled "Yes!"

<u>Grief being the love or emotional involvement expressed by a mourner is the over-riding, grief-</u>

<u>changing insight of this book</u>. All other insights shared with me by the grief experts sent into my life (such as Ken) fall under the umbrella of love expressed by a mourner. I believe the truth that *Grief Is Another Expression of Love and Love Never Dies* trumps all excuses for avoiding grief. Here are a few of the common excuses for avoiding grief that I hear from clients:

- **Expressing my grief emotions shows weakness or a lack of faith.** No, expressing grief is healthy. Mourning and expressing your grief are signs to others you need help and support. Expressing grief purges you of potentially dangerous emotions and physical toxins produced by your body in reaction to the stresses of grief.

- **Giving into grief and expressing it just makes me sadder and doesn't make anything better.** This is not true. Expressing grief releases emotional tension and results in emotional healing and a sense of physical well-being.

- **There is nothing that I or anyone else can do or say to change things. It will always be this way.** Maybe your situation won't change, but sharing your grief story, thoughts and feelings can change how you perceive your grief and yourself. Given time and space for healing, you can change and heal in your grief.

- **I don't want to cry (lose control, break down, fall to pieces, lose it) in front of others.** (By the way, the correct term for all of these phrases is "grief outburst" which sounds much healthier and more acceptable.) You need others' support during grief. If they don't know you are struggling with your grief, how do they know to be there for you? Crying and expressing the painful, uncomfortable emotions of grief signals others that you require comfort and support.

- **My loved one wouldn't want me to grieve.** Your loved one may have asked you not to mourn after he or she dies, but that is an unfair request. If it were possible for us to visit our own funerals, we would most likely be upset if no one was crying. Mourners not crying at a funeral would send the message that the person who died is not loved or had not impacted anyone else's life. Show your love for the person and grieve in a healthy way. He or she deserves to be missed.

- **I shouldn't be sad. I should be happy for my loved one** (They are in a better place. They are no longer suffering, etc.) Yes, they are in a better place or they are not suffering, but you still miss them. It is healthy and natural to be sad or even depressed over the death of someone who is significant to you. You do not severely miss the loss of a mere acquaintance, but you do dearly miss the loss of a valued, treasured relationship. Your loved one is worthy of your grief.

- **No one has time or wants to hear my problems.** You need others and you need a support system during grief. You were not meant to go through this dark, difficult time by yourself. Seek out people who love you, sincerely care about your well being and will listen without judging or giving unsolicited advice.

- **I don't want to be a burden to others.** In life everyone has times that they need to give support and encouragement to others and times when they need to receive support and encouragement from others. Grief is your time to receive help from others graciously.

- **No one will allow me to grieve.** Express your grief in places that you feel safe and with people who make you feel safe and cared for. Spend as little time as possible with those people who just have no clue what mourners need.

- **My grief comes from my selfishness in wanting my loved one back.** Think of your grief as a huge emotional wound that needs care in order to heal. If you had a huge physical wound that required regular attention, it would be ridiculous for others to shame you for the time you spend in changing a dressing on the wound as being selfish. Taking care of your grief needs is self-care, not being selfish.
As a man of faith, I believe that we are made in the image of God who is a relational being. In fact, He is His own community (Father, Son and Holy Spirit).
   God describes Himself as "jealous" meaning that He prizes His relationship with us. He wants nothing or no one to take that relationship from Him. We mourners prize our relationship with the person who has died. Therefore, we grieve

when that relationship is changed by the death of the one we love.

- **I refuse to have a pity party for myself.** How can you not feel sorrow for yourself at the loss of someone who you loved and meant so much to you? These are valuable people who deserve remembrance and honor through your expressed healthy grief emotions. Believe it or not, sometimes in life it is healthy to be sad, depressed or filled with regrets. The acknowledgment and expression of these painful emotions in grief leads to healing.

- **I am a private person when it comes to feelings.** Grief does not always let you pick your time and place to mourn. Grief outbursts can strike unexpectedly. Don't avoid grief. When a grief outburst occurs, see it as an opportunity to actively show your continued love for the person. If you feel more comfortable mourning in private, excuse yourself and go somewhere alone if you can.

- **I don't have time for grief.** Grief emotions demand your time and your attention. When strong grief emotions are suppressed or denied, they will come out anyway. Many times these suppressed or unaddressed emotions come out in ways that are unhealthy, inappropriate and destructive.

- **Once I give into grief I will not be able to get out of it.** No. Usually the more intense the initial grief expression, the more the struggle with grief emotions will lessen over time.

- **If I have the right perspective, there is no need to struggle with grief.** No one is exempt from grief and its emotions no matter what their worldview, background, culture or beliefs. These factors will shape how you mourn, but you will still need to mourn. How you mourn is up to you.

- **Since I am a Christian and I believe that I will see my loved one again, I don't need to grieve.** This belief can be the cause of guilt for many mourners. No one is exempt from grief and its emotions no matter what his or her religion and beliefs are. These factors will affect how you mourn, but you still have the need to mourn. A strong faith can provide the mourner with additional resources to help and support him or her during the grief journey.

- **I should celebrate and not be sad because my loved one is in a new home and freed from suffering in this world.** The time after the death of a loved one can be a reason to feel joy for your loved one in light of your faith and beliefs. It is healthy and appropriate to miss someone who is important to you. In fact, sadness at their death can be a display of respect and honor for the loved one.

- **Death is part of life. I just need to forget and get over it.** Death is part of life, but grief is also a fact of life resulting from life, dying and death. You need the transition of grief to help you accept your new reality of life without the physical presence of the one who died. As for "getting over it," grief is not a case of the measles. I hate to give you bad news, but there is no "getting over" grief. There can be change and healing though. Grief is the continued and needed expression of love for these important and missed people.

- **No one can help me because no one has the same type of loss and situation that I have.** There are no two griefs that are exactly alike, but all human beings have lost or will lose someone to death. Although others may not share the same details or particulars of your unique grief, you do share two things in common with other mourners-you love the person and you miss him or her. Mourners with different types of losses can find comfort and support from each other.

There may be countless other excuses that mourners give for trying to avoid the experience of grief, but they are just that-excuses. As a fellow mourner, I can tell you that my loved ones and yours are good people who had an impact on us and countless others. They need to be shown honor and respect. The stories of their lives and influence need to be told and retold. We show others how valuable and worthy these loved ones are when we take time in our lives to continue to remember them and to express our love for them.

<u>**Grief is never easy, but it is often as complex and overwhelming as the mourner perceives it to be.**</u> In our culture many mourners view grief as an odious, inevitable reality which is to be dreaded, feared, contained or avoided. No wonder countless grievers suffer

with what others label as complicated, prolonged or pathological grief.

When grief is seen for what it is – another expression of the love the mourner has for the person who died and an opportunity to choose to maintain a meaningful relationship with that loved one – the burden of grief can be lightened.

Blessed are those who mourn, for they will be comforted. (Matthew 5:4 NIV)

NOTE TO READER: What if I did not "love" the person who died?

Every person with whom we have a relationship has an influence on us. Some affect our lives in a positive way while others can have a negative or destructive impact. Many of these people we can be emotionally tied to in our relationships may not be loveable people. Still they did and do have many times an effect on our lives and who we are.

Grief provides us an opportunity to deal with the death of someone we love or in whom we have an emotional investment. That grief also allows us to take a personal inventory to determine how the death impacts us. The resulting grief impact inventory can permit us to see the person's life in the context of how they shaped who we are and what we can become.

Often the deaths of difficult people in our lives can cause us to go through regrets, guilt or a longing for the ideal relationship that we had always wished for with that person. With his or her death, the hope for an opportunity to resolve our imperfect relationship has died also.

It is only after taking time to mourn and to complete a grief impact inventory that we can determine how we will make sense of our relationship with the one who has died. That grief impact inventory can also help us determine what we want our lives to be without that person physically present. The ultimate goal of mourning for either someone significant in our lives that we loved or did not love is to accept the losses involved and adapt in a healthy manner to life without that person in our presence.

CHAPTER THREE

WHEN YOU HEAL, YOU HURT

How many mourners have started their grief journey only to stop when the process of dealing with grief thoughts, experiences and emotions becomes too painful? Would they have continued their progress toward healing in grief if they had only had someone there to cheer them on? Would they have stayed the course of their grief journey if they had known that hope and healing were just around the corner and within reach?

The morning after my first session of a grief support group.

I had wanted to stay at home in bed all day, but I couldn't. I had two children to take to school and a paycheck to earn. I had awakened that morning with a horrible headache, a dark depression and a deep despair that was worse than I had ever experienced.

Forget that stupid grief support group last night. I am not going back. I had expected these "group people" to make me feel better, but instead I was disappointed and angry the next day. Sitting in my office nearly twelve hours post group, I felt twice as bad as

I did before entering that circle of mourners agonizing over their losses.

My supervisor popped into my office doorway, smiled and asked, "How was the support group last night?" I thanked him again for referring me to the group. Then I explained how the group that he had suggested was one of the worst experiences of my life. I told him in detail how bad I felt and how this group was just not for me. I am not proud to say that in my emotional state then I may have included a few expletives deleted to define and punctuate my rage and disgust. Years later I understand that under all that anger were my fears and feelings of hopelessness.

You have to understand my boss was two things: an encourager and an eternal optimist. My grief temper tantrum that morning was not going to dissuade him from being present to comfort me in my pain. He hung in there even in the face of my furious protests of how my life was deteriorating after the deaths of my wife and daughter.

I can say the following statement because I have been and still am a person in grief. People going through grief are some of the most difficult people to support and help. Many mourners early in grief are not able to hear or accept comfort due to the unspeakable pain they endure. Thank goodness there are people like my old boss who did not take my rejection and berating of his attempts to help me as personal attacks.

Calmly my supervisor told me that maybe the group was not for me, but that I needed to give the sessions a chance to work. "Of course, you hurt this morning, "he said, "Last night for the first time since your accident you exposed feelings and emotional wounds that need to be addressed. When you hurt in grief, the pain experienced shows that you are beginning to heal."

I hated to admit that what my boss said made sense. As I sat in silence and in the sadness enveloping me, he asked that I go to at least two more sessions before giving up on the group. I did. After completing the six week group, I attended two more grief support groups in the area. My supervisor had been right. I needed to acknowledge and sort out the painful emotions of my grief in order to start healing. Obviously the grief support groups worked for me. For the last twelve years I have facilitated similar grief support groups and witnessed hundreds of mourners start healing by acknowledging and expressing their pain.

How many mourners have started their grief journey only to stop when the process of dealing with grief thoughts, experiences and emotions becomes too painful? Would they have continued their progress toward healing in grief if they had only had someone there to cheer them on? Would they have stayed the course of their grief journey if they had known that hope and healing were just around the corner and within reach?

Mourners who choose to avoid grief are paralyzed by the pain of the moment. They give into the myths of our Western culture that pain of any kind is unacceptable at any level and at any time. They truly believe that they should never hurt. When the going gets difficult and painful and there is any possible escape, they give up and bolt.

One sweet woman who had come to the first session of a grief support group that I was facilitating stood up just minutes into the meeting and declared, "This is just too painful!" She darted from the room and was in the parking lot starting her car before any of the stunned members of the group could respond. No one could comprehend what had motivated such a sudden, extraordinary reaction. All that I had done before her abrupt departure was to welcome and congratulate the participants for being brave enough to show up.

This sudden, painful exit proves that Sigmund Freud was right. Freud said that people run toward pleasure and run away from pain. I think Freud's statement is definitely a no brainer, but I will give him credit for stating the obvious. No person seeks out pain; they avoid it at all costs. Most mourners use the same tactics when pain looms ahead in their grief journey. They run from pain, avoid pain and deny pain.

Pain serves a purpose. Physical pain protects the person by signaling that something is wrong and needs to be addressed now. Emotional pain in grief does the same for the mourner. Pain seeks to protect the mourner's well being and emotional safety by indicating that some aspect of the person needs attention and special care. Pain in grief is also a signal that mental, emotional and spiritual healing have begun.

Mourners who avoid the pain of grief and short circuit their own healing have been unable to realize the insight that is the big paradox of grief: *In order to heal, you must hurt.* In other words, pain is a sign or the harbinger of progress, hope and healing in grief.

Bereavement counselors and their clients can tell you from personal experiences that suppressing, avoiding or denying strong grief emotions for a long period of time can have disastrous results. Dr. Alan Wolfelt, director of the Center for Loss and Life Transition, refers to this grief never acknowledged, examined and expressed in healthy ways as "carried grief." (Wolfelt, 2007. *Living in the Shadow of the Ghosts of Your Grief,* Companion Press)

When mourners avoid and run from the painful realities of loss, they carry unreconciled grief with them

throughout their lives. The results can be ruined relationships, careers and lives. Often by not dealing with
the painful emotions of grief, people put their emotional, mental, physical and spiritual well being in jeop-
ardy. The sad truth is that avoiding the pain of grief of
the moment can produce ongoing pain throughout a
lifetime.

Mourners can shorten their difficult grief struggles
by acknowledging their emotions and finding ways to
release the emotional tension inside them. The choice
of how to acknowledge and deal with grief emotions is
the responsibility of each mourner. Not every mourner
will need to attend grief support groups or grief counseling in order to do this. Each mourner must choose
how to deal with their grief emotions in a healthy way.
Creating and depending upon a good social support
system and healthy coping skills that are meaningful to
the individual mourner can be a good start to healthy
mourning.

There are many consequences to unacknowledged
and unexpressed grief emotions, but all the outcomes
can fit into two probabilities. The person refusing to
deal with painful grief emotions will either explode or
implode. If the person explodes, the suppressed painful
emotions under pressure become a geyser of mis-
directed anger and destruction. The potential results
of this explosion are a loss of self-control and self-
esteem; lost friends, relationships and careers; and
lost physical, mental and emotional health. The irony
is that by avoiding the painful emotions of the moment,
the mourner can set the stage for ongoing pain-filled
losses in his or her life.

If the person avoiding grief's pain implodes, the
suppressed emotions cause the mourner to collapse
from within. We used to call these emotional implo-

sions "nervous breakdowns." Once strong leaders of families, businesses, churches and communities fall apart unexpectedly and without warning before our eyes. We found these sudden emotional implosions hard to believe.

The truth is that these emotional implosions or "nervous breakdowns" were rarely sudden. The inward emotional collapse of the person avoiding painful emotions had taken time. The suppressed emotions had slowly become corrosive toxins eating away at the persons' delicate mental and emotional infrastructure. The irony of many of these emotional implosions was that the mourner trying to stay strong and "hold it together" was slowly crumbling from within.

When I think of mourners who have avoided grief and imploded emotionally, my thoughts go immediately to my mother who died in 2007 from breast cancer at the age of 76. Mother was not a stranger to loss and grief. At the age of 19, she lost her 46-year-old mother who died of breast cancer. My grandmother died just months after my birth. In her early twenties my mother's first daughter, my younger sister, became ill and died while still an infant. My mother rarely talked about my sister, the details of her life or her death. To this day I don't know exactly what claimed her life.

Once I asked my mother how I could possibly endure the painful struggle after the deaths of my wife and daughter. I thought maybe with her past losses and life experience that she might have some wisdom or good advice to help me. She sighed and said, "You have to do what I do. I just don't think about it."

Now as an adult mourner and student of grief I understand more about my mother's mourning than I did as a child under her care. I now understand the days that she locked herself in her bedroom. She spent those bad times lying on her bed with the shades drawn, and complaining of migraines. My mother had imploded.

The message for mourners in all this is "If you want to progress and heal, expect pain and discomfort." Mourners find this message difficult to hear and accept. The unspeakable pain of the moment can make them question if they have the ability or the desire to endure grief.

You and other mourners can take heart and claim power for dealing with the pain from what has worked for others in grief. When mourners see other mourners farther in their grief walk doing well, they can realize that there is hope for them to effectively travel through grief and its pain. Suddenly there is hope for the mourner doubting their ability to endure painful moments.

How mourners see their grief experiences and the resulting painful emotions can either cause them to run from grief or to stand firm and endure. Understanding the true nature, purpose and possible outcomes of the grief process arms the mourner with a confidence to face painful moments.

UNDERSTANDING THE FIVE BASIC PRINCIPLES OF GRIEF:

PRINCIPLE # 1:
Grief is the natural response to loss.
What you experience in grief after the death of a loved one is absolutely natural to human beings. Grief is the love or emotional investment expressed for the person who died. So in your struggle with the pain of the moment you can be comforted that you are not suffering an abnormal emotional, mental, spiritual or physical state that needs to be cured or corrected.

Often mourners feel that no one else can understand what they are going through. There are some common emotions and experiences to which the majority of mourners can relate. These shared emotions and experiences can give you the individual mourner an encouraging message that you have the power to endure the pain of grief if fellow mourners have endured their pain.

You can find strength to endure the emotional pain of the moment if you understand what you feel is a natural human response and a continued expression of the love and emotions you have for the one who died. The relationship with your loved one has not died; it has just changed and can be maintained. The pain of the moment is well worth bearing to be able to carry your loved one into the future with you.

PRINCIPLE # 2:
Emotions experienced during grief are neither good nor bad. They just are.
One reason that many mourners avoid the painful emotions of grief is because they fear the loss of control and rationality that seem to happen when they allow themselves to experience uncomfortable, demanding emotions. Let's state the obvious. Control is an illusion. We think we have control in our lives until something we would not choose happens - such as the death of a loved one.

No one controls their grief emotions. Who would choose the unpleasant, uncomfortable and often painful feelings of sadness, depression, anger, guilt or regret? Yet these can be part of a healthy grief experience.

If grief has a purpose as an emotional transition toward healing, then maybe the emotions of grief have purpose also. Grief emotions could be helping us to become reflective, to process grief and to take a detailed inventory of how the loss has impacted us. With that inventory we are equipped with valuable information that will help us to choose our path toward joy and healing.

PRINCIPLE # 3:
Grief emotions will be dealt with...now or later.
No matter what the mourner does he or she cannot escape painful emotions after the death of a loved one. Remember the last time you were on your cell phone and a child tried to get your attention? That child was relentless. No matter how much you passionately gestured and mouthed that you were on the phone, that child needing your attention did not give up. They got your attention.

Grief emotions will not be denied. They are relentless and will be dealt with now or later. Again no one controls or chooses their emotions, especially during grief. Think of a huge cauldron with a fire going under it. If the logs in the fire suddenly break, the flames surge around the cauldron. Then everything on the bottom of the pot boils up to the top. Grief emotions are the same way. When a loved one dies, the uncomfortable, unpleasant and painful emotions of grief boil to the top. Mourners can't always control or choose what they feel.

Although mourners cannot select their emotions, they can determine how they respond to grief and its pain. Mourners are not powerless victims of grief. They are empowered with the choice of responding in ways that are healthy, appropriate, and constructive. These choices can position them to endure the pain of grief and to progress toward health and healing.

How a mourner chooses to deal with his or her grief emotions should fit the needs, personality and grief style of the individual mourner. Emotive mourners should be allowed to openly express their powerful grief emotions in safe places with safe people (those who make the mourner feel comfortable and cared for).

Stoic mourners need to grieve differently. Forcing a stoic to "open up" in front of others about their grief emotions can cause additional trauma. Stoic mourners need to acknowledge their emotions and grief experience in a safe, comfortable method for them. The stoic usually chooses to process grief and to vent emotions by (1) thinking through the experience or (2) working through the emotions in physical activity.

PRINCIPLE # 4:
Grief is an individualized experience. Everyone does not grieve in the same predictable way.
The individual mourner's grief is shaped primarily by the one-of-a-kind, unique in all the universe relationship that they had with their loved one. Therefore, every mourner's grief is different and unique although there are commonalities or shared experiences among mourners.

No one formula, recipe, set of rules, therapy or solution for surviving grief fits all. With the support of other mourners, the individual has to navigate his or her way through his or her own unique grief. First though the individual mourner has to acknowledge, experience and process their very personal grief emotions. The only way to survive is not to avoid grief and its pain, but to go through it.

PRINCIPLE # 5:

Grief will not always be like it is in the beginning. As time passes, the grief experience changes.

This basic principle of grief can give the mourner a reason to hope. In the beginning of grief there is a very intense emotional pain. Initially grief emotions and pain can be overwhelming and all-consuming. For the person new to grief, everything in their life can be a memory of the devastating loss. Desperate mourners often ask, "Will I <u>ever</u> feel joy again?"

The good news for mourners is that over time grief and pain change. Time does not heal all wounds, but time gives opportunities for the mourner and his or her grief to change and become different. Does it get better? Better is not the right word. Different describes the nature of grief as it changes.

The best example I can give is my own personal grief experience. Several years have passed since the deaths of my wife Cindy and my daughter Katie. There is not a day that goes by even now when I don't think about them. I still miss them today and mourn their deaths, but my grief is different now than it was just after the accident. My grief has changed all the way to today...from one year after the accident, five years after, ten years after, fifteen years after. My belief, prayer and hope are that my grief and I will continue to change moving toward reconciling my losses and toward my healing.

Because I have witnessed mourners who have suffered and lived their grief well, I can be hopeful for me and you as mourners. The same hope that I am experiencing in my grief can happen for you. The first step toward this hope and healing is to decide to face and experience grief for the full journey. There will be times that you question your decision and your sanity, but if you keep giving the grief process another chance you can be rewarded with joy, hope and peace of mind.

When will you as a mourner be able to feel joy again? When will you realize that you are progressing in your grief? When will you know that you have fully engaged with life once again? I don't know exactly when all of these things will happen for you, but I am convinced that they can happen.

I remember vividly how that moment of healing realization happened for me. One day I walked outside and suddenly I felt as if "the clouds had parted and the sun was shining into my soul." For the first time in a long while I felt more like the old Larry. I knew that everything including me and my life remained changed forever by my losses and my grief, but suddenly I knew with certainty that I could get up every morning with a reason, a purpose and a hope.

Dear mourner, I cannot say when and where this can happen for you. I can promise based on my personal experience and the experiences of fellow mourners that it can and does happen.

"...In this world you will have trouble. But take heart! I have overcome the world." (John 16:33b NIV)

NOTE TO READER: If I decide to attend a grief support group, what can I expect?

Every grief support group will vary in its make-up, format and specific goals. Some groups are closed groups that have a scheduled beginning and end. Once the group has started, no new members are added. These groups last a specific number of sessions and are usually very structured in order to cover a set curriculum in the lifespan of that specific group (usually 6-8 weeks). These groups are designed to educate group members, to allow participants time to share their personal experiences and to give group members a good start to their grief journey.

Other grief support groups are open and on-going. This type of group has scheduled meeting times- maybe weekly, twice a month or monthly. The format of this group is usually a more casual, less restrictive one that allows members to attend as frequently and as long as the participants feel a need for the support provided. In these groups there is no consistent, predictable group composition from session to session. New and old members come and go. Group participants attending receive grief education, more opportunities and time to share their experiences and sometimes the mentorship of fellow mourners who are deeper into their grief journeys.

When looking for a group, here are some good questions to ask:

- <u>What are the dates, times, location and duration of the group?</u> If you have missed out on a current session, ask when the next group will be offered and how often the groups are offered. If an upcoming group fits your schedule and needs, ask if you can be placed on a waiting list to reserve a place in the next group.
- <u>How many participants will be in the group?</u> Most group facilitators agree that a group of eight to twelve is most beneficial and productive for the support group members. When the group grows to more than twelve to fifteen members, it is more of a class than a group. The smaller the group is,

the more time that is available for individuals to share personal experiences and feelings.

- Who is sponsoring this group? Knowing the sponsor of the group can give you some hints as to the approach the group facilitators will take in leading the group. Example: A church-sponsored group may take a faith-based, religious approach to grief and loss. This may or may not fit what you are looking for to meet your needs as a mourner. Another example: A grief support group sponsored by an agency that specializes in cancer or Alzheimer's disease may specialize in mourners who have lost loved ones to specific diseases or causes.
- Who will be facilitating the grief support group? What are the group facilitators' credentials or training for leading the group? Group facilitators can be lay counselors or licensed professional therapists. Are the facilitators required to go through training in order to lead the groups? Do licensed therapists supervise the lay facilitator(s) and the groups? Another question that is important to some mourners is if the facilitators have a personal history of loss.
- Is this group limited to specific types of losses or open to all types of losses? Some grief support groups specialize in the type of loss such as loss of a spouse or loss of a child. Most grief support groups are open to any type of loss due to any cause of death. Be aware that some grief support groups take participants who have experienced any type of loss such as divorce, loss of a job, and pet loss.
- Are there requirements mourners must meet in order to attend the support group? Some groups

require their participants to go through a registration or application process. This can include an interview (by phone or in person), an evaluation and an orientation to the group process. Some groups also require that the mourner must wait two months or more after the loss before participating in the group.

- <u>Are there any fees or costs for participation in the grief support group?</u> Some groups charge for the materials provided and the services of the group facilitator.

  You might want to ask if there is a one-time fee or a per session fee. You might also want to ask if you will be required to purchase workbooks or other supplies in order to participate.

- <u>Are follow up services provided after the group ends?</u> Many closed groups will offer additional services in order to provide any on-going support the group participant might need. Ask if you will be provided with additional grief support or grief counseling resources.

- <u>Remember that grief support groups provide support, not therapy or grief counseling.</u> If you feel that you may need more in-depth, personal support and help for your loss, you might consider entering into individual grief counseling with a licensed professional.

- <u>Ask about the structure of the group and if there are any rules to help give you an idea of what to expect in your first grief group session.</u> Most grief support groups have rules in order to help the participants and group facilitators to know what to expect from each other in sessions. (See Grief Support Rules below for an example of what the support group may require for rules of conduct during sessions. Remember that this set of rules is only an example of what I ask my group members to remember.)

GRIEF SUPPORT GROUP RULES

In order to help each group member benefit from the six sessions you will attend, we ask that you remember the following strong suggestions:

1. **_Attend all sessions._**
   The grief support sessions are designed to be a progressive learning experience.
   Each session builds upon the next. If you miss a session, you will cheat yourself of the full experience. You will also cheat other group members from hearing what you might have to share.

2. **_Be on time and stay for the entire session._**
   Our time together is limited and your participation helps you and your fellow group members.

3. **_Do your assigned grief work outside the group sessions._**
   The "homework" given for outside the group sessions will allow you to use what you have heard in the group and to promote better group interactions. You are an adult, and you have the choice of doing or not doing the weekly out-of-group assignments.
   Don't spend more than 20-30 minutes total on each exercise. Those who have done the exercises in past groups have shared how the exercises enhanced their group experience and their healing process.

4. **_Keep what you hear in the group._**
   The group must be a safe place where members are free to express themselves without fear of being judged or of being quoted to anyone outside the group. Keep everything that is shared in the group CONFIDENTIAL.

5. **_Respect everyone's need to participate._**
   Share what is necessary to discuss with the group remembering that other members have important items to share also. Be brief.

6. **_Respect everyone's unique grief._**
   Don't give into the temptation to compare another's grief with yours. Everyone has their particular grief and their own unique way of coping with the pain of loss. This is not a contest to see who has it worse or better.

7. **_Respect everyone's right to their personal feelings and beliefs._**
   Avoid judging others' emotions, beliefs or motives.

8. **_Be supportive of each other._**
   The group is here to listen, to encourage and to companion each other through their grief, not to judge or give advice.

9. **_Remember everyone in this group is doing the best they know how._**
   Getting through grief is a matter of using coping skills that do not hurt the mourner or anyone around him or her.

10. **<u>Remember that we are all works in progress.</u>**
    Be patient with every member in the group. Create
    an atmosphere of trust.

CHAPTER FOUR

WHAT CRYING IS LIKE

When the overwhelming sadness of loss is finally acknowledged and let out, the doorway is cleared to address the multitude of other emotions waiting behind that sadness. Sadness, anger, fear, guilt, regrets and countless other emotions are parts of processing grief and healing.

In a grief support group session.

Jim leaned forward into the grief support group circle. Tears built up in his eyes. His voice cracked slightly as he said in a husky whisper, "You have to realize that I have never cried openly in front of anyone at any time. My family or friends have never seen me cry over anything... until now."

Jim and his wife Angela had just started coming to the grief support group that I facilitated. Their sixteen year old daughter Chelsea had died from leukemia just four days before Thanksgiving.

Jim continued, "Now I am crying eight, nine, ten times a day. I can't control or stop it. My wife was just about to call a psychiatrist to set an appointment for me. But then I figured this grief and crying thing out.

I am okay with the crying now…now that I know what crying is like." Jim's head dropped, tears struck the floor in front of him and there was a shared silence.

All of the support group leaned toward the weeping West Texan as I asked, "And Jim, what *is* crying like?"

Jim's head raised and his hands wiped across his face. "Crying is like puking."

"What?" I said in a startled whisper to this odd comparison.

Jim put his hands palms down on his pant legs as he leaned back, looked at me with a smile and said, "Crying is like puking. It feels bad while you're doing it, but it feels so good when you get everything out."

That was a turning point for Jim in his mourning and a learning experience for me as a counselor. Jim's discovery about his crying and grief has stuck with me over the years. He had realized that the cliché that real men don't cry was a myth—especially in grief. I had learned a rather crude, but effective explanation of the true nature and purpose of crying.

Traditionally most men are stoics in dealing with grief. Women are generally emotive mourners. Stoics are in sharp contrast to emotives who are compelled to express their feelings in order to purge themselves of difficult and painful emotions or thoughts.

Stoics feel uncomfortable in expressing their emotions without restraint. They deal with grief in one of two ways. First, they might process their grief emotions by intellectualizing or thinking through their grief. Often counselors talk about men needing solitude— to go to their "cave" alone to brood, think and evaluate their emotional wounds. Second, stoic mourners might become busy or active to expend and cope with their emotional tension.

A good example of a stoic man finding release for emotional stress can be found in many old Western movies. The scene closes as some traumatic event takes place. The event could be the death of a family member or friend. The following scene opens with a close-up of an axe striking a log and then opening to a wider view of our stoic hero feverishly chopping firewood. The family didn't need the extra firewood. The stoic needed a strenuous, physical activity that would help him find release for the emotional tension within him and to focus on a plan for what to do next.

Let's go back to Jim and his insight about crying in grief. Jim had realized that his crying served a purpose. In giving himself permission to feel and express his sadness, Jim was purging himself of the multitude of grief emotions inside of him. From now on Jim would not see his crying as a problem or a weakness, but as a healthy release.

Despite the crudeness of Jim's explanation of how crying works in grief, I have shared his apt description with hundreds of mourners and they all get it. They have been there in their personal grief outbursts and can understand the release and relief that often results from crying and openly expressing emotions.

No mourner should be forced or expected to be an emotive griever if that is contradictory to his or her personality or grief comfort zone. Sometimes additional emotional trauma can be inflicted upon the mourner when a comforter is not mindful of letting the mourner make his or her own choices on how to release the emotional tension of their grief.

My daughter had a running joke with me on the grief support group nights that I came home to my children. After a session of listening to fellow mourners' stories and painful emotions, I was usually worn out emotionally and physically. "Well, Dad," she would say with a smile. "Did you do your job tonight? Did you make 'em cry?"

I smiled back and replied, "No, dear, I didn't make them cry. But if they needed to, I let them."

From watching other mourners such as Jim and his wife Angela I have learned that crying in grief for many mourners can be the start of a healing expression of many other difficult emotions. When the overwhelming sadness of loss is finally acknowledged and let out, the doorway is cleared to address the multitude of other emotions waiting behind that sadness. Sadness, anger, fear, guilt, regrets and countless other emotions are parts of processing grief and healing. They are all important parts of the transition from life with the person to life without him or her present.

Grief and its emotions make mourners stop and take stock of their lives after the loss. Only after determining how the death of their loved one has impacted them can mourners be prepared to map out what to do next in their grief. In his book *The Other Side of Sadness* George Bonanno of Columbia University cites research that shows that sad people are more reflective, seem more detail-oriented and perform better on memory tests. (Bonanno, 2010. Basic Books) Could it be that sadness equips mourners for the necessary grief inventory to make wise choices in their grief? Could it also be that the emotions accompanying sadness facilitate the grief inventory process and healing for the mourner?

In our culture we complicate mourning often by judging the amount of crying or emotional outbursts we observe. If the mourner is crying and being openly expressive, we might say that obviously they are not handling their grief well. We are making the assumption that crying is being out of control and irrational. This assumption is untrue. The release of emotions is healthy grief and a sign of a mourner meeting his or her personal needs in grief.

If we never see the mourner cry, we can often wonder to ourselves if their relationship with the person who died was close at all. In that conclusion we are assuming that a lack of emotional display or crying is the same as a lack of love. That assumption can be untrue depending upon the person, the relationship and the progress of the mourner in their grief. You may just have caught the mourner on a day in which grief was not the main task or focus for the day.

Most mourners worry how others view their crying or grief outbursts. Almost every time a counseling client or grief support group member cries in front of me, they grab for a tissue, dab their eyes and apologize. I tell them the crying is okay by saying, "Hey, you're sad so you cry. If you can't cry here with a grief counselor, where can you cry?"

Most mourners would choose not to cry in front of others for fear of losing "control." None of us mourners has control over everything that happens in our life. We were not given a choice about our grief and its emotional consequences, but we are empowered with the choices of how we deal with death, loss and the emotions we experience.

We mourners have two options. We can suppress the painful grief emotions welling up inside us or we can find healthy ways to acknowledge and express or release grief emotions and the distress they cause. Crying can help let the emotions and the distress out.

Not only do the tears of grief let the sadness and other emotions out, they serve another purpose. Emotional tears are chemically different from tears that result because of an eye irritation. Emotional tears contain more protein and beta-endorphin, one of the body's natural pain relievers. In addition the tears of grief expel toxic chemicals produced by the body under emotional stress. Tears ease the pain of grief and rid the body of chemicals that can cause physical destruction and life-threatening diseases.

Once Jim saw his grief and his crying as having purpose, his grief burden was lightened. Therefore, grief, crying and emotional expression are to be embraced and worked through, not to be avoided or fought. His grief struggle was not ended, but diminished slightly. Once Jim dispelled the myths of grief, crying and the release of pent up emotions, he gained the courage to move toward healing.

Other prevailing myths about grief and how to deal with it are plaguing many mourners and complicating their progress in grief. See if you recognize any of these common myths of grief.

COMMON MYTHS ABOUT GRIEF

MYTH # 1:

Grief is a negative experience which must be gotten over quickly. Life must go on. Truth: Grief is a natural, appropriate reaction to loss. Grief gives the individual time to do self-evaluation and to reconcile themselves to the change in the relationship with the person who has died. The only way to get through grief is to experience and cope with it. Embracing grief and its painful emotions leads to healing. In grief and loss, emotions are neither good nor bad. They just exist.

MYTH # 2:

Mourners are best left alone to grieve. Truth: Occasional solitude can be helpful for mourners. To be alone with your thoughts now and then can be helpful. Mourners need opportunities to share their memories and receive comfort from others. Community and support systems play an important part in a healthy grief journey.

MYTH # 3:

Giving into grief and its emotions shows weakness, a lack of faith or spiritual strength. Truth: All people, whatever their religious or spiritual beliefs or practices, experience grief at the loss of a valued loved one. Spiritual and religious beliefs can be a comfort and can provide additional resources to ease mourning, but they cannot completely eliminate grief or the pain of loss.

MYTH # 4:

Grief is a predictable process and takes place in successive stages. Truth: Although common emotions and grief tasks toward healing are experienced by all mourners, grief is not a linear, predictable process. Grief is a progressive, individualized journey to healing.

The often cited grief stages of Denial, Anger, Bargaining, Depression and Acceptance have led mourners and many caregivers to think of grief as following a set pattern or predictable steps that must be followed exactly toward healing. These stages were developed by Dr. Elisabeth Kubler-Ross, a death education pioneer, originally as five stages experienced by dying patients. (Kubler-Ross & Kessler, 2005. *On Grief and Grieving, Simon and Shuster)* Although mourners go through similar experiences in grief, there is no one blueprint or map for the path through grief.

MYTH # 5:

Grief can finally end. Truth: Time gives people an opportunity to heal and to learn new coping skills, but the process and pain of grief can last a life time. The good news is that the intense mourning period immediately following the loss does not have to last a lifetime. Grief and the mourner change over time.

The closeness of the relationship with the person lost determines the difficulty of the grieving process. We grieve for lost loved ones in direct proportion to the love and emotional investment we have in our relationship with them.

MYTH # 6:

Individuals must grieve in appropriate ways and places. Truth: When I hear this myth I think people are actually advising mourners to grieve as quietly as possible and as far away as possible from them. Sometimes the "comforters" surrounding the mourner are uncomfortable with outward signs of grief. "Comforters" are many times pained at seeing mourners hurt and at a loss for what to do. Out of their discomfort with the mourner, they may suggest that more appropriate grief expressions and places might work out better.

Often grief and its accompanying emotions are uncontrollable and demand to be expressed. Mourners are advised to grieve in places where they feel safe and with people who make them feel comfortable and supported.

MYTH # 7:

Grief is an emotional reaction. Truth: Grief is a process involving the entire person. Therefore, grief has physical, mental, emotional, spiritual and social aspects. Mourning meets deep needs of the person in all these areas. It is an exhausting process that demands the full resources of the mourner.

MYTH # 8:

Mourners must "let go" or "detach" from their lost loved one. Truth: Mourners cannot let go of the people they love. They can learn to accept the reality of the death, its impact on their lives and the loss of their relationship with the loved one as it was. They can maintain a loving, healthy and healing relationship with the one who died.

MYTH # 9:

Only family members and close friends grieve. Truth: Everyone who feels an attachment to the deceased experiences loss.

MYTH # 10:

People just grieve loss caused by deaths. Truth: All losses are grieved. In fact, we spend a good portion of our lives mourning what psychologists call "small deaths," losses caused by crises and life changes.

MYTH # 11:

Loss is a perfect opportunity to teach important lessons about life and death, sin and punishment, faith and eternal rewards. Truth: Loss provides us an opportunity to minister to people's most intimate needs. A mourner can always learn throughout the grief process, but a good lesson about life and death is not what they most often need initially. In their darkest times of grief, mourners need support, encouragement, comfort and hope.

Ignoring, suppressing, avoiding or denying sadness and the other grief emotions can certainly endanger and damage the mourner's well-being or the mourner's relationships, career and future. We have talked about mourners who do not address the feelings and pain of loss as suffering either an emotional explosion or implosion. By avoiding the truth that grief emotions must be acknowledged and purged, mourners put their physical, mental, emotional and spiritual health in danger.

Stockpiling unexpressed emotions in grief has another consequence. Fearful mourners seeking to escape their painful, uncomfortable emotions bring an abrupt end to any progress on their journey toward healing, joy and peace of mind. Mourners have short circuited their own grief.

Often the coping skills we mourners utilize in order to save ourselves from pain result in pain of another kind. Often the mourner wants only to avoid entering into the threatening dark valley of grief emotions that confronts him or her. At that point he or she cannot see that the dark valley of grief is a passage to the light of hope and healing on the other side. Ironically their unhealthy ways of dealing with grief and its pain push them into a deep, dark emotional pit where they are stuck and helpless to escape.

What Mourners Do To Short Circuit
Their Grief Progress:

There are four common defense mechanisms that mourners employ that can short circuit healthy grief. All of these coping skills if used to take a brief vacation or break from the overwhelming demands of grief can be healthy and effective. You as a mourner cannot mourn intensely 24 hours a day, seven days a week. Taking a short respite from grief occasionally can be healthy.

If any of these defense mechanisms are used by the mourner to escape completely the work of confronting and processing grief emotions, the grief process becomes short-circuited and the mourner becomes stuck in their journey.

- **Denial** is a defense mechanism that can protect mourners from uncomfortable, painful grief emotions. This coping skill is commonly an early part of grief which allows us mourners to accept as much of the painful new reality as we can tolerate at that moment.

  Denial can give us a break from the hard work of grief. An extended period of denial though hides us from reality, keeps us from acknowledging our grief, expressing it, coping in a healthy manner and healing our grief wounds.

- **Suppression** of grief is "stuffing your feelings, "keeping a stiff upper lip," "staying strong for others' or any other action in which we mourners do not allow ourselves to express or cope with powerful emotions resulting from the loss. Grief emotions will be dealt with now or later. If later, the unaddressed emotions may come out in destructive ways.

• **Running** from grief is keeping busy or filling your life with other interests to escape the reality of the loss and the impact it has on the mourner's life. Becoming a workaholic, submerging your time and efforts in social and church activities, or focusing on others and their grief are prime examples of running. The problem with running is that when the mourner stops to rest, the grief and its impact are still there.

Some of the worst advice given to us mourners is to become busy with a filled schedule and forget the loss. That busyness only delays the inevitability of having to adapt to the consequences of the loss of a loved one.

• **Avoiding** grief is refusing to deal with those things that remind us of our loss in any way. When we mourners use this defense mechanism, we refuse to talk about the death or its consequences at all. Extreme avoidance can cause us to withdraw from people, places and things that were once of great interest, but are now just painful reminders of our pain and loss.

AS A MOURNER YOU HAVE A NEED AND A RIGHT TO EXPRESS YOUR GRIEF. THE PERSON WHO DIED IS PRICELESS TO YOU, TO OTHERS AND TO GOD.

YOU HAVE PERMISSION TO MOURN THE LOSS OF SOMEONE VALUABLE AND TO SEARCH FOR

A NEW WAY TO LIVE AND MOURN. YOU CAN LIVE AND MOURN WELL IN ORDER TO HONOR HIS OR HER MEMORY AND TO HONOR GOD'S GIFT TO YOU OF THE RELATIONSHIP WITH THE PERSON WHO DIED.

GIVE EXPRESSION TO YOUR LOVE AND YOUR GRIEF EMOTIONS EITHER IN WORDS OR ACTIONS. MAKE THOSE GRIEF EXPRESSIONS PRODUCTIVE AND MEANINGFUL FOR YOU AND OTHERS. YOU OWE IT TO YOUR LOVED ONE AND TO YOURSELF.

When Jesus saw her weeping, and the Jews who had come along with her also weeping, he was deeply moved in spirit and troubled. "Where have you laid him?" he asked.

"Come and see, Lord," they replied.

Jesus wept. Then the Jews said, "See how he loved him!"

(Jesus' reaction to the death of Lazarus and to those mourning the loss of Lazarus. Moments later Jesus raised Lazarus from the dead. John 9: 33-36 TNIV)

NOTE TO READER: What if I don't cry enough or don't cry at all? Is that abnormal or unhealthy?

In the past the predominate belief in grief support groups and counseling was that being openly expressive and crying without restraint was the most healthy way to vent grief emotions. Emotives who openly express their grief emotions were praised in grief support groups and sometimes held up as the model for every mourner to follow.

These beliefs caused a lot of professional and lay counselors to try to force stoic grievers to become emotive grievers. This made stoics believe that there was something inherently wrong with them and their coping skills. Stoics under such pressure can feel discouraged and incapable to grieve in the "right way." This situation often short-circuited their grief and healing.

There is no one right way to grieve. There is not just one right way to vent the pressure of grief emotions and move toward healing. The stoic and the emotive can successfully acknowledge and vent their emotions in different and still acceptable ways. The emotive's style of venting is easily observed. The stoic's style of emotional venting is more personal and hidden. Both can be healthy.

Every grief is different; every mourner is different. So the measure of health in grief is not style but the results, progress and healing that take place.

My two children mourned the deaths of their mother and sister in different ways. My daughter Sarah was the emotive talking to me often about her feelings. We spent many times crying together. My son Christian was the stoic teenage male. I don't remember him crying in front of me at the funeral or after. When I acted as the caring, concerned father asking him how or what he felt emotionally, he became even more stoic and silent. Often the answer I got from him was, "I don't feel anything."

Years after the accident, I found out indirectly that Christian had been doing his mourning on his own terms. I got a call from his high school counselor to say how proud she was of Christian over the last semester. She shared with me that my stoic son had acted as a co-facilitator with her in a grief support group for students who had recently lost a loved one.

I was thrilled to find out that Christian was dealing with his loss in such a healthy way. With that news, I learned that even though my son and I are different in our mourning styles, we both chose to use our grief experience to reach out and help others. **Crying in grief is not mandatory.**

CHAPTER FIVE

YOU HAVE TO FIGHT FOR YOUR RIGHT TO MOURN

But please, can't we stop making mourners believe that they need to hurry up and get over their grief? Can we stop making mourners think that they have a mental or emotion disorder if they do not finish their intense grief on our timetable? Can we stop causing them to feel that remembering their loved one, feeling a twinge of pain and crying years afterward is unhealthy and abnormal?

Another grief support group. The session has already begun.

Beverly was beaming and seemed to be impatient as she waited for her turn to share the news of her past week between sessions with other members of the grief support group. Beverly had come to the group three months after the death of her 79 year old mother Ellen. Her mother had died after a long struggle with Alzheimer's Disease. Beverly, an only child, had been her mother's caregiver for almost six years.

Beverly moved forward and nodded her head as I said her name and asked how her past week had been. "I have had a very hard week, but a good one. Remember last week how you said that we have the need to grieve our loved one, and we don't need anyone else's permission to do so?"

"Right. All mourners have the need to remember and memorialize their loved one on a continuing basis," I replied.

"Well, last week I remembered what you had said because my husband had forbidden me to come to this group at all. He thinks that the best way for me to deal with my mother's death is to grieve briefly and get over it," Beverly said her lips tightening and her face becoming red with anger.

"My husband had even told me after we came home from the funeral three months ago that I had six weeks to grieve and that he didn't want to hear any more about my mother after that," said Ellen's only child. She continued with determination in her voice, "Well, I told him last week that he had no right to tell me to never mention my mother again. I told him that I still loved her, missed her and needed to keep her memory alive. I told him I didn't need his permission to come to the support group and grieve for my mother in a healthy way. That's what I told him. And he hasn't been on my case about my mother since then."

Beverly smiled at the group. All of us sat in awe and silence as we witnessed a turning point in our fellow mourner's grief journey. As a counselor I had known and stated the right and need to express grief to hundreds of clients. I had never realized until Beverly was in my group that sometimes as a mourner you have to fight for your right to mourn your loss.

Our death denying culture continues to send the message to mourners that the healthiness of an individual's grief is to be measured by how quickly and proficiently the mourner "gets over" the loss and moves into a productive life. I remember my co-worker who was supported by our employer while her husband went through months of chemotherapy to fight cancer. Once her husband died and weeks passed, she was fired because of a lack of productivity.

The wells of compassion for this mourner had gone dry when her grief continued too long. Unfortunately this example is typical of our culture and the corporate, bottom-line world. In our competitive, achievement-oriented culture, grief and mourners are seen as inefficient.

The average leave for bereavement in the business world is three days. THREE DAYS of leave are allowed only if the person who died is a member of the employee's immediate family. If a grandparent, aunt, uncle, other distant family member or friend dies, no official bereavement leave is given. The mourner takes vacation days or time off without pay for those losses. "Prolonged" grief and lowered productivity beyond a specific "normal and acceptable grief" period in the workplace are often seen as malingering, pathological and a reason for termination.

Please excuse me while I get up onto my soapbox for just a second.

My opinions and this book are not going to change the average bereavement leave in the United States. In fact, after over thirty years of the existence of hospice which deals daily with death, dying and bereavement, the average bereavement leave for a hospice worker remains three days.

But please, can't we stop making mourners believe that they need to hurry up and get over their grief? Can we stop making mourners think that they have a mental or emotional disorder if they do not finish their intense grief on our timetable? Can we stop causing them to feel that remembering their loved one, feeling a twinge of pain and crying years after the death is unhealthy and abnormal?

Over sixty years have passed since the deaths of thousands that occurred in the bombing of Pearl Harbor. Each year in December, crowds still gather at the Pearl Harbor Memorial in Hawaii and cry over the deaths of brave young men killed there. Does anyone walk up and say, "Oh, come on. It has been over *sixty years* since these people died. When are you weaklings going to get over it?"

Nearly ten years have passed since the attack on 9/11. Each day thousands come to Ground Zero in New York City and cry over the almost 3,000 people killed there. Does any bystander walk up and say, "Oh, come on. It has been *ten years* since these people died. When are you cry babies going to get over it?"

No one tells these Pearl Harbor and 9/11 mourners not to cry and not to grieve for two important reasons. The first reason is that those who died are important people whose lives need to be remembered. The second reason is that these are losses and historic days to be remembered because our world was never the same afterward.

Well, guess what? My loss and your loss are our very own personal Pearl Harbors and 9/11's. The people we lost to death are just as important to us as those who died at Pearl Harbor and on 9/11 are to those who continue to remember them.

After our losses, our personal worlds will never be the same—just like the bereaved of Pearl Harbor and 9/11. Therefore, we as mourners will continue to remember our loved ones and the days that they left our lives for the sake of our natural, healthy mourning.

If our mourning bothers the bystanders observing our grief, we mourners are not the ones who need to "get over it." The judges of our grief and its duration are the ones who need to "get over" their clueless, uninformed evaluation of our personal grief. We mourners say this with all due respect to those trying to get us to stop mourning. We are not going to apologize for the discomfort or inconvenience that others experience watching us mourn in a healthy way.

Okay, I'll step down from my soapbox now.

I am sorry if my views seem a little harsh, but too many mourners starting their life path into healthy mourning and healing have their grief short-circuited by our culture. The problem is that our society considers talk about death and grief as morbid and taboo. Living in an atmosphere where grief emotions and mourning are stifled we mourners sometimes feel forced to carry unexpressed grief and unresolved issues concerning a loss throughout our lives.

Most friends and advisors around the mourner give advice with one of two goals in mind. First, well-intentioned advisors want to comfort the mourner out of his or her grief. Everyone hates to see another person in pain. We naturally want to fix the person and make everything all right. Mourners are not broken, and they cannot be fixed or set straight by platitudes, inspirational thoughts and unsolicited advice. Often mourners are in too much pain to be able to hear the comfort in these attempts to influence their grief. Mourners want to be heard and have their stories and experiences affirmed rather than solved or judged.

Second, advisors around the mourner actively seek to shut down the grief process because they do not understand or empathize with the mourner's need to remember, to experience grief, to adapt to a new reality and to heal. These advisors include the well-intentioned and the uninformed that simply do not know what to do with mourning people. These advisors also include those who do not want to be reminded of the harsh truths of dying, death and bereavement. The majority of our society knows that they all will die and that they all will say good bye to loved ones in this life. They simply do not want to be reminded of those facts. The open expression of grief reminds them of death's inevitability.

The truth is that life lived with the end in view can lead to a more fulfilling and meaningful existence. Just ask philosophy students about Existentialism which builds upon that fact. The wisdom writings of the Old Testament talk about living life with Death in mind by saying, "It is better to go to a house of mourning than to go to a house of feasting, for death is the destiny of everyone; the living should take this to heart." (Ecclesiastes 7:2 NIV).

Experiencing the death of someone we love causes us mourners to review our beliefs and our personal understanding of death, dying and loss. Our loss experience can cause us to prepare for our inevitable end and for the life which still lies ahead for us. When our grief is short-circuited, we are robbed of the possibilities of navigating grief in a healthy fashion and of seeing life and death with a meaningful perspective.

If you are going to stand up for your rights as a healthy mourner, then maybe you should know what those rights are.

As A Mourner.....

- **You have the right to grieve in your own way as long as you don't ruin your life or others.** Results or progress in grief are more important than style. It doesn't matter if you are openly expressive or stoic in venting your grief emotions. You should be able to feel safe to acknowledge your feelings and to find a constructive, healthy release for the emotional tension within you.

- **<u>You have the right to talk about your loved one whenever you feel like talking.</u>** Speaking about your loved one and saying his or her name out loud allows you to vent grief emotions. Talking about your loved one can bring you comfort or keep the memories of the person alive for you.

  Don't let the people around you dictate how you mourn. At the same time, remember that there are safe and unsafe places to openly mourn. There are also safe and unsafe people with whom you can express yourself. Choose your people and places wisely without stifling your grief.

  Also keep in mind when you share about your loved one in front of others that they may have a different mourning style. Don't be insulted if they choose not to join with you in the conversation or share about the loved one at that moment. You can sometimes cause other mourners unnecessary pain by trying to force them to mourn like you do.

- **<u>You have the right to express your feelings.</u>** Your healthy grief is more important than the feelings or opinions of those who maybe do not understand how grief works or what you need. Supportive comforters listen without judging or giving unsolicited advice.

- **You have the right to remember and honor your loved one on a regular basis.** You have an on-going need to remember your loved one in healthy and meaningful ways. This on-going need is not fully met in a one-time funeral or memorial. You can choose your rituals to meet this need to remember the loved one in light of your specific needs, beliefs and personality. (See Your Rights in Remembering Your Loved One later in this chapter.)

- **You have the right to be upset about normal, everyday problems.** This means you are free to have a bad day or a bad moment and the world will not end. Feelings are fickle and change from one moment to the next. One moment you can be having the best day ever since the death. Then suddenly a memory or situation can send you as a mourner into what feels like the worst day or moment you have ever experienced.

    Be patient with yourself when a bad moment or day happens. *But please, never use your bad day or a bad moment as an excuse for hurting or mistreating others.*

- **You have the right to question why the person died.** Asking the "why" and "What if" questions is part of grief. We mourners are trying to make sense out of something that doesn't make sense to us—the loss of a loved one. Just remember: there may not be any answers to these questions.

    Once you have asked these initial questions, then you can move onto the more important question of "What now?" in your grief journey.

- **You have the right to ask God the hard questions.** A review or evaluation of your belief system can be a natural part of your grief. Sometimes we determine that the rules in life are not what we thought they were.

  Sometimes we determine that our vision of how God works in this world is not valid. Questioning God and our belief system is not a lack of faith. It is an opportunity to strengthen or correct what we believe to be the truths of life, dying, death and loss.

- **You have the right to occasional grief outbursts.** In grief and in life, we describe our experiences as up's and down's. When you openly express your grief, you are not "losing it" or "falling to pieces." You are expressing your feelings in a healing, healthy way. Having grief outbursts can be necessary and healthy.

- **You have the right to ask others for help.** Most comforters may be completely clueless as to how to help us as mourners. If you don't let others know what you want, you probably will not get what you need. Remember that it is not a sign of weakness to ask for help. Requesting help is a sign of being healthy and realizing that you can mourn better with the assistance of caring, compassionate people around you.

Your Need To Remember:
Since mourners have the on-going need to remember in significant ways their loved one, they can call upon their own experiences and imagina-

tion to create rituals to help them do that. The following list describes the mourner's rights to shape the rituals they use to meet their specific needs to memorialize the loved one in meaningful ways.

Your Rights in Remembering
Your Loved One

1. You have the right to make use of rituals.
When we cannot find words to express our grief emotions, rituals help. Ceremonies for remembering loved ones help us acknowledge the importance of the people in our lives and our need to reflect upon how these people changed us.

2. You have the right to create events of remembrance that will meet your unique needs.
Your loved one is unique and the grieving needs of you and your family are unique. Do not be afraid to add personal touches to the ritual to express the special qualities of the loved one and to address your family's special needs of remembering the loved one.

3. You have the right to ask supportive friends and family members to be involved.
Ask others to participate at a level at which they feel comfortable. Don't force, demand or manipulate others into participating. When a variety of people contribute to a ceremony, the ritual honors everyone's memory of the loved one.

I remember one bereaved parent who was deeply insulted when other family members refused to participate in an impromptu memorial service to a family member who had died two years earlier. The problem was that the family was not given any notice that they would be asked to participate in such a ritual. Remember: don't try to force friends or family to mourn just like you.

4. **You have the freedom to create your own grief experience or traditions.**
Everyone mourns in their own way. Don't let tradition or others dictate how you memorialize your loved one. If the ceremony or action is meaningful to you, then it is right for you. Being creative and loving will produce a one of a kind ceremony honoring your loved one.

5. **You have the right to embrace and express your pain.**
Memories can and do stir up grief emotions. Acknowledging and expressing your grief during and after a ceremony are part of your healing process. Don't be ashamed to cry. Find listeners who will accept your feelings no matter what they are.

Remember, the memorial or funeral does not mark the "closure" of your grief. The ceremonies are the beginning of a healthy grief journey which over time will change but never completely end. As long as you love and miss the person, you will need to find ways to express these feelings.

6. **You have the right to plan rituals that reflect your religious faith and beliefs.**
Your faith incorporated into the ceremony can be a source of additional comfort in your grief.

Expressing that faith can be a reminder of those things that inspire and support you.

7. **You have the right for a continuing search for meaning before, during and after the rituals.**
Questioning your faith or the very meaning of life after the death of a loved one is not a sign of weakness, but a symptom of healthy grieving. Don't let others stifle your search for meaning. Funerals, memorials and rituals do not bring an end to your grief or your search for meaning.

8. **You have the right to make use of memory during the events.**
Memories are an important part of the legacies that exist after the death of someone loved. Make these legacies a prominent part of the memorial. Give others the opportunity to share their memories if they feel comfortable doing so.

9. **You have the right to be mindful and careful of your physical and emotional limits.**
Respect what your body and mind are telling you as feelings of loss and sadness leave you fatigued. Remembering your loved one in a meaningful way is important, but your overall health is very important. Get rest, eat well, exercise sensibly and pamper yourself.

10. **You have the right to move toward your grief and heal.**
While the ritual or ceremony is a one-time event, your grief is an on-going process. Reconciling your grief will not happen quickly. Be patient and tolerant with yourself. Avoid people who are

impatient or intolerant of your needs to mourn in a healthy manner. Neither you nor those around you must forget that the death of someone loved will bring other changes and possible losses into your life.

Mourners and the comforters around them often ask how long grief lasts. Some grief experts and counselors say six months to a year normally. If the grief is complicated, they might say maybe it could last two to four years. But these timetables for grief are misleading. The grief experts are describing the intense, overwhelming portion of grief right after the loss. I say that this intense part of grief takes as long as it takes. Your grief is on its own timetable no matter what the experts say.

Mourners, please know that if you have lost a significant person in your life that you will miss them always and grieve at some level. Also know though that time spent in remembering your loved one and mourning is time well spent as long as it doesn't hurt you or anyone else. Your loved one is an important person whose life and legacy need to be remembered and honored on a regular basis.

Time spent in healthy mourning is time spent honoring your loved one by living a good life. A hospice chaplain friend of mine reminded family members attending a funeral service that they were more than just a list of people in the obituary under the heading of "survived by." He challenged each family member to see themselves as "living memorials" to the life and memory of their loved one.

Don't give into the pressure of society and others to hurry up and get over your loss. Fight for your right to mourn a valuable person who is no longer in your life.

For everything there is a season, a time for every activity under heaven.
A time to be born and a time to die. A time to plant and a time to harvest.
A time to kill and a time to heal. A time to tear down and a time to build up.
A time to cry and a time to laugh. A time to grieve and a time to dance.
(Ecclesiastes 3:1-4 NLV)

NOTE TO READER: When do you know the grief displayed by a mourner is unhealthy?

There are cases where the coping skills a mourner is using to deal with his or her grief become destructive and unhealthy to the mourner and others around them. An unhealthy mourning style can be indicated when the observed mourning negatively affects for a duration of time such factors as:

- The mourner's ability to function in everyday, necessary tasks at home, at work or in social settings
- The quality of the mourner's lifestyle
- The mental and emotional wellbeing of the mourner
- The physical wellbeing of the mourner
- The stability and strength of important relationships in the mourner's life
- The ability of the mourner to make continued progress in moving toward reconciliation of his or her grief

Sustained difficulties in one or a combination of these areas can indicate that the mourner is in need of additional support or help. Professional help may be indicated depending upon the severity of the difficulties.

Although each grief is unique to the individual there are common emotions or experiences that can be shared among the majority of mourners. (See Common Reactions in Grief in the next chapter for a list of these natural responses to grief.)

Please remember there is no <u>one</u> way to mourn and heal. Each individual mourner will vary in what natural reactions in grief they personally experience. There is no one set of rules for how to navigate through grief in a healthy way. There are only suggestions based on the commonly held experiences and feelings of a majority of mourners.

Every grief is complicated in its own way. There are certain aspects of every grief that cause the individual mourner to struggle. Complicated grief generally refers to when mourners make no progress or become stuck in their grief. There are two types of complicated grief generally speaking. The first type is when there are no observable signs of grief or progress being made. Often observers watching a mourner with this complicated grief would not even know this person had suffered a loss.

The second type involves the hyper-exaggeration of a natural grief response. This might be uncontrollable crying, wailing, and physical reactions displayed usually only during the initial period after a loved one's death. The difference is in complicated grief this uncontrollable reaction often happens each time the mourner re-visits the loss.

Again, another factor in determining complicated grief is when the mourner appears to be making no progress in his or her grief. Sustained arrested grief progress indicates a mourner may need professional help and support.

Here is a good thought to keep in mind for friends and caregivers viewing mourning behavior that they find troubling. The determination or diagnosis of unhealthy or complicated grief should be left to professional caregivers and mental health professionals.

Do not rely upon assumptions reached by what you subjectively deem as unhealthy or abnormal mourning behavior from personal experience. Many times well-meaning comforters and caregivers around mourners can cause additional emotional trauma by mislabeling a mourner as abnormal, unhealthy or inappropriate.

CHAPTER SIX

YOU DON'T HAVE
TO MOURN ALONE

Mourners of all ages often have the belief that they are different from everyone else. Their loss is so unique that it makes them one of a kind. They feel alone in their crisis and that no one can possibly understand or help them. This condition is called "terminal uniqueness." When mourners discover that others have experienced common emotions and experiences in grief, terminal uniqueness fades. Mourners in the company of fellow mourners can lighten each others' grief load.

In the main meeting room of GriefWorks, a children's grief support ministry in Dallas, Texas.

Another busy night of activities for the family members at GriefWorks was coming to an end. The parents of the mourning children and teens had just completed their adult group session. They were waiting anxiously for their children to emerge from their group rooms. Theresa was especially anxious to see her six year old son Chad after his group tonight.

You need to know that this was Chad's and Theresa's first GriefWorks session. They had come to

GriefWorks only the week prior for an evaluation and orientation to the program after the death of Chad's father and Theresa's husband of fifteen years. From his initial entrance into GriefWorks for that orientation until his arrival for his group tonight, Chad had made it known to everyone that he did not need to be here. He did not like being forced to attend.

Theresa had been firm and loving with Chad throughout all his resistance to participating at GriefWorks. She had expressed her fears that maybe she was causing her only child further trauma by forcing him into the group. She had shared with the adult group that after his father's death, Chad had become angry, unruly and obnoxious at home and at school. What scared her most she told the group was that Chad refused to talk about his father with her or anyone else.

The door to the young children's group swung open, and the first child out was Chad. He looked around for his mother and ran toward her with his arms open to hug her. She bent down and Chad jumped into her arms smiling and pressing his cheek to hers. As he smiled, Chad exclaimed, "Guess what, Mom? I met two boys in my group and their fathers have died too!"

Young Chad had learned something that night that mourners of all ages find out when they attend grief support groups and bereavement activities: "I am not alone!" For Chad and his worried mother that insight of not being different and no longer being all alone was a turning point in their grief journey.

Mourners of all ages often have the belief that they are different from everyone else. Their loss is so unique that it makes them one of a kind. They feel alone in their crisis and that no one can possibly understand or help them. This condition is called "terminal uniqueness."

When mourners discover that others have experienced common emotions and experiences in grief, terminal uniqueness fades. Mourners in the company of fellow mourners can lighten each others' grief load.

In each grief support group that I facilitate, I hand out a list of common reactions in grief. My purpose is to show mourners that there are a variety of responses that can take place in grief and all of them can be natural and healthy.

There have been many responses from group members reading the list such as "I could add a few new reactions to your list" or "If I have a reaction not on the list, does that mean I need to worry?" The most memorable question I have been asked came from a widow whose eyes widened as she read through the reactions. She looked toward me with worry on her face and asked, "Do you mean I have to have all of these to be normal?"

The list is not exhaustive. These are the most common cited by mourners, but it does not cover all possibilities. Mourners may recognize themselves in some of the items and hopefully realize that no matter how strange and bizarre their grief response may seem to them, they can still fall into the category of "normal." Just like Chad, none of us mourners likes feeling different or all alone.

It is not unusual for mourners to feel that they are going crazy in their grief. The reason mourners can question their sanity is that they probably have never experienced a loss like the one with which they are struggling. The mourners are in new emotional territory. They are experiencing feelings and thinking thoughts that are foreign and overwhelming to them.

In counseling or in grief support groups, clients will stop after describing a grief thought or behavior and say, "I guess that sounds crazy. Right?"

I tell them, "No that sounds fairly normal. Just keep talking. I'll tell you when it gets crazy."

As you review this list, remind yourself that if you are progressing through grief without hurting yourself or anyone else, you are responding to grief naturally. You are healthy and not alone.

Common Reactions in Grief

Grief can be a highly emotional state, but it influences far more than just the emotional part of the mourner. Grief affects the whole person. It is a natural, appropriate human response to loss that impacts the person mentally, physically, socially, emotionally and spiritually.

Grief is the continued expression of the love for the person who has died. People experiencing loss often notice that they are so radically changed that they feel like there must be something wrong with them. In the majority of cases, mourners are experiencing common responses to loss. These reactions can include:

MENTALLY:

- **The inability to be excited or motivated to do the things that need to be done.** In the beginning of grief there is a lethargy or lack of energy to do any activity. In addition to the lethargy, there can be apathy about almost every activity or aspect of life that used to bring joy to the mourner. After the loss of a loved one, mourners can feel that their identity and purpose in life have also been lost. Life without identity and purpose can produce a "Whatever!" attitude in the mourner.

- **Experiencing difficulty in problem-solving or making decisions (feeling like you are in a fog).** The mourner can feel as if what is happening to them and around them is unreal. One grief support group member said, "I feel like I am watching a movie about someone else's life. I just cannot bring myself to accept that she has really died!"

- **Suffering a lack of concentration.** Mourners find themselves unable to read, watch television or stay focused on one task for any length of time. Their minds become restless jumping from one idea to the next.

- **Becoming forgetful.** Mourners lock themselves out of their homes and cars repeatedly. They miss standing appointments and meetings. They lose track of keys, important papers and even simple everyday items. Bills often go unpaid because payment deadlines come and go. Often mourners find it difficult even to remember what day it is.

  Mourners can help themselves by making lists, keeping appointment books, leaving keys and other items in assigned places and surrounding themselves with understanding people who can help them when they forget important dates, times, people and obligations.

- **Experiencing impaired judgment (doing things or making decisions that just don't**

make sense). Mourners can be considered impaired in their thought processes and focus. Often during the first year grief counselors advise mourners to not make any major life-changing decisions without extensive research and feedback from their support system.

- **Mental exhaustion.** Frequently mourners complain that they are so tired that they do not have the power to think. This exhaustion is the result of all the mourner's resources being poured into dealing with the loss and its consequences. Rest and self-care are important to help reserve energy and to contend with fatigue.

- **Feeling restless.** Mourners are unable to sit still. This physical activity is mirroring what is happening in their mind. They are moving from place to place in the house just like their mind wandering without purpose from one thought to another.

- **Feelings of helplessness and hopelessness.** Depression is a common part of grief. Mourners feel helpless because nothing they do seems to change their situation. They also feel hopeless in that they realize that the loss is permanent and will never be fixed. The good news is that the depression experienced in grief is short term usually and not chronic.

- **Experiencing an unending sense of gloom.** Sadness and an overwhelming negativity seem to hang over mourners. There is a tendency to be more pessimistic. For mourners already prone to being negative and suffering from depression this can make the gloom even darker and more oppressive.

- **A preoccupation with the deceased person and their image.** The mourner yearns so much to see the loved one just one more time. This yearning causes the mind to play tricks on the mourner. There can be the feeling that someone they see on the street looks just like the loved one until they come into focus. There can also be the relentless feeling that at any moment the loved one will knock at the door or walk around the corner.

PHYSICALLY

- **Being more susceptible to colds, flu and other physical ailments.** Because grief is a stressor, the mourner's life runs on adrenaline. This stress compromises the immune system and makes the mourner vulnerable to illness.

  Mourners would be wise to see their physician to check out physical ailments that they may suffer during grief. Don't write off an unexplained pain or malady as just part of the stress of grief. Have a physician check it out thoroughly. Most counselors recommend a mourning person have a full physical exam within six months to a year after the death of the loved one.

- **Being unable to sleep or sleeping all the time.** Grief can cause mourners to develop insomnia. Mourners can also sleep too much in order to escape the painful experience of grief. If sleeping patterns change drastically in grief, the mourner should consult a physician for help. Lack of sleep is a major red flag for mourners and their counselors. Not getting good quality sleep can cause additional complications.

- **Changes in eating habits.** Some mourners lose their appetite during grief. They need to remind themselves to eat and drink in sufficient amounts even though they may not feel hungry or thirsty.

  Other mourners may be stress eaters who find comfort in food. Again the mourner needs to be mindful of his or her tendency to overeat and to maintain a healthy diet and exercise schedule even when they feel they don't have the energy to do either.

- **Physical symptoms such as tightness in the throat or heaviness in the chest.** Psychosomatic pain and ailments are not unusual in the mourner. The mental, emotional and spiritual anguish and anxiety of grief can be the cause of many real or imagined physical distress or pain. Mourners need to check with their physician any time physical pain or discomfort happen.

- **Constant fatigue.** Grief takes a lot of energy. Mourning can drain the grief-stricken person emotionally, physically, mentally, spiritually and socially.

- **Avoiding social contact and activities.** Mourners often withdraw into their shells just when they really need to be with others and experience social support. No mourner should try to go through grief alone.

- **Fearful of being alone.** When a loved one dies, the mourner feels insecure and vulnerable. The world no longer seems like a safe place.

- **Afraid to leave the home and fearful of staying alone in the house.** Mourners often have multiple, contradictory feelings at once. This mixture of emotions can make the mourner confused and disoriented.

- **Afraid to go to sleep (being alone at night with your thoughts).** Nights and bedtime can be difficult for mourners. Often the mourner may find it helpful to develop a routine to prepare for sleep. That routine can often include reading or journaling at the end of a difficult day.

- **Feeling the need to tell and retell the experience of the loved one's death (in detail).** Often mourners feel compelled to share their story and experiences repeatedly. Many grief experts believe it may be the mourner trying to make sense of the experience and put it into context. Usually over time the way the person tells the story will change giving an indication of their progress in the grief journey.

- **Feeling they must suppress their thoughts and feelings about the loved one in order to protect family members or to keep others from feeling uncomfortable or sad.** Mourners protect others' feelings, especially family members, by not talking about the loved one or their grief. This habit can lead to the proverbial elephant in the living room that no one talks about. The result is no one in the household mourns in a healthy way.

- **Blaming others for your loss, your feelings or your circumstances.** Mourners may feel the need to find someone or something as the cause of their loss and grief experience. This blame can be used as an excuse to not work through or process their grief. Often these blaming mourners see themselves as healthy and everyone else as having a problem.

- **Resentment toward others whose lives and families continue as normal.** Mourners can feel resentment to others who have what they see as perfect, intact families. The resentment of course rises from their anger that their lives and families will never be the same again.

EMOTIONALLY

- **Anger toward others or the deceased.** Anger is simply not liking how things are or wanting them to be different. This is a natural and justified feeling in grief. Mourners can express this anger toward others and the deceased simply because they need a target for this uncomfortable, unsettling emotion. However anger can be acknowledged and expressed in constructive rather than destructive ways.

- **Guilt for not being able to protect or save their loved one.** We human beings second guess almost every decision we make. The same second guessing happens in the death of a loved one and the grief that follows.

  In the deaths of my wife and daughter, I have reviewed every detail leading up to the accident and what followed. I was the father and husband. So I should have been able to protect my family. Why didn't I? What if I had only insisted that I drive rather than my wife? If so, would she be alive and me dead? If only I had been able to delay our drive by even a few minutes that day, could we have avoided the accident? If only I had suggested another route for our trip, would I have all of my family still with me? The questions, doubt and guilt went on and on.

  A mourner has every right to feel any emotion that occurs in his or her grief, even guilt. Thanks go to my comforters who listened to me, held their tongues and did not tell me that I had no reason to feel guilty. They allowed me to process my guilt, determine if it was real or imagined, and to forgive myself for my shortcomings.

- **Regrets for things done or not done.** Mourners can express many regrets: that they never said good bye, that they didn't say "I love you" enough, or that they didn't say "I'm sorry" and "Please forgive me." Mourners must process these regrets, determine if they are valid and extend forgiveness to others and themselves.

- **Mood changes over small events.** Mourners' feelings place them on an emotional rollercoaster that has them almost always irritable, easily frustrated and easily upset. Often the small, insignificant events that trigger an emotional outburst are just the straw that broke the camel's back. Their emotional outburst is a grief outburst that has been building up over time.

- **Finding no joy (or reason) in once pleasurable activities.** Counselors have a term for the inability to experience joy. The word is "anhedonia." Mourners can experience anhedonia due to the overwhelming pain and stress of grief. Often the mourner has lost the feeling of purpose and is surviving from moment to moment. The mourner finds it difficult to see any reason for joy, happiness or peace of mind. The mourner can also feel that any experience of joy is a betrayal to their loved one. They have the mistaken belief that honoring their loved one means always being sad and somber.

- **Emotionally fatigued or depressed.** Depression is a common part of grief. In fact there is a type of situational grief which is called grief depression. Depression in grief is usually short in duration. If the depression becomes chronic, the mourner should seek professional help. Many times prescription drugs can be helpful as long as they don't cover up feelings or keep the mourner from doing his or her mourning. Usually anti-depressants coupled with counseling are helpful for the depressed mourner.

- **Unpredictable or uncontrollable crying.** These periods of crying are usually healthy grief outbursts. Mourners should allow grief to happen when they feel it. They should always mourn in safe places with safe people who make them feel comfortable and cared for.

- **Bitterness.** This is anger taken to an unhealthy extreme. Anger held onto long enough without being expressed or resolved can become resentment. Resentment held onto and fed by the angry mourner can turn to bitterness which can do untold damage to the mourner and his or her life as well as to those around them.

SPIRITUALLY

- **Inability to find consolation in your faith.** Sometimes the pain of grief is so overwhelming that the mourner cannot hear or feel the comfort extended to him or her by others. In my mourning, I became so tired of comforters quoting Romans 8:28 to me. *"We know that everything works together for good for those who love God."* They were trying to let me know everything was going to be all right with God's help. I believed the verse and I believed that God would help me and my family. In my unspeakable pain of grief though, I was unable to find solace in the scripture at that moment.

  In the Bible, the patriarch and man of faith Jacob refused to be comforted over the perceived death of his son Joseph. When his eleven other sons showed him Jacob's blood-soaked coat, nothing that any would-be comforter did or said could make Jacob feel better. Jacob told his family that his grief over his treasured child would follow him to his grave.

Then Jacob tore his clothes, put on sackcloth and mourned for his son many days. All his sons and daughters came to comfort him, but he refused to be comforted. "No," he said, "I will continue to mourn until I join my son in the grave." So his father wept for him. (Genesis 37: 33-34 NIV)

- **Inability to pray to God.** Many mourners have shared with me that they no longer pray to God after their loss. They think that obviously their prayers to God for the safety or healing of a loved one were useless.

    I encourage mourners to not cut off all communications with God or long held connections to their faith. I tell them when they feel up to it that they can share their feelings with their Heavenly Father. They can talk about their loss and their disappointment with God in a truthful and reverent manner. When they do, they join the ranks of many giants of faith in scripture who have voiced disappointment with God's action or inaction in their lives. (Just read through the Psalms and Lamentations to see what I mean. In the New Testament James praises the patient, enduring Job who sometimes questioned God's actions-James 5:10.)

    I encourage mourners upset with God to tell Him about their pain and their thoughts on what has happened to them for two important reasons. First, God appreciates His children speaking to him from an honest heart. Second, God is like any other father. He enjoys communications from His children on a regular basis. Unlike earthly fathers though God the perfect Father patiently hears and understands fully what we feel and why.

- **Crying in church services.** In the emotionally charged experience of worship, the mourner is touched deeply in his or her soul. Feelings suppressed at other times come bubbling up to the surface. Being in church, being surrounded by supportive fellow believers, hearing music that stirs memories and listening to the inspirational allow the mourner opportunities to express his or her deepest beliefs and to vent grief emotions.

- **Anger toward God.** I can never forget a statement made by the facilitator of the second grief support group I attended early in my grief. He started off by saying, "I want you to feel free to express whatever you feel. If you're angry, tell us. And if you're angry at God, tell us and Him. He already knows anyway."

  That was a light bulb moment for me. I suppose that I had thought there was this secret compartment in my brain where my thoughts were shielded from God's sight. I immediately thought to God and to myself, "Yeah, I am angry with you, God." I quickly added, "Now I don't want to be, but I am." From that moment on, I felt freed and safe to express in a healthy way any emotion that I felt.

  Years later in prayer to God I was brought to my knees with a second confession of anger toward my Heavenly Father. I realized at that moment that I was not only upset with God for taking Cindy and Katie physically out of my life, but I was also angered at Him for leaving me here to live and grieve. In my mind, it would have been much better for God to take my entire family to Heaven to be together with Him.

I tell you mourners about my anger toward God for one reason. I told God I was angry at Him not just once but twice. I wasn't struck with lightning, and He continues to bless me and my family. God knows how you and I feel as mourners and why. I believe God gave us grief and all its emotions to help us transition through the losses He knows we will experience. He is a loving, understanding, merciful and forgiving Father who wants you to heal. Mourners, speak to God from an honest and sincere heart. Let Him know how you feel and let Him help you heal.

Rejoice with those who rejoice; mourn with those who mourn. (Romans 12:15 TNIV)

CHAPTER SEVEN

TO GET HELP
ASK FOR HELP

We mourners expect family and friends to be mind readers or psychics divining precisely what we need. We think to ourselves, "They love us and they know what we are going through. So why wouldn't they just understand and give us what we need to get through grief?"

October-November 2007 in my counseling office.

As far as my client Jerry was concerned if they took the months of November and December out of the calendar, he would not have missed those days at all. You see, Jerry's wife Sheila lived for the holiday season. That was her favorite time of the year. In fact, every January 1st Sheila was already planning her gift list for that year's Christmas.

Going through the first few years of holiday seasons after his wife's death was absolute torture for Jerry. Every year he looked at the calendar and dreaded the days leading up to family gatherings without Sheila present. Every year he experienced an increasing resentment that his family and friends forced him to do Thanksgiving and Christmas as normal. Jerry felt his life had changed forever, but Thanksgiving, Christmas and all the days of the year still happened as if nothing had changed.

Jerry told me in counseling sessions that he was angry at the world during the holidays. "Everyone has their family intact, and the holidays remind me that my family can never be the same. But my kids expect it and they should have Thanksgiving and Christmas just like every other kid. They just don't have their mother to enjoy it with them. We miss her so much!" Jerry had said through clenched teeth.

In a session one week before Thanksgiving I asked Jerry what his plans for the holidays were. "Oh, we'll be doing the holidays different this year," Jerry answered. "I told my sister how painful doing the holidays is for me."

I was shocked. In the last session Jerry had vented for almost the entire fifty minutes on his resentment toward his family and their traditional holiday celebrations. Still he refused at that time to ruin everyone's holiday by telling his family how he felt. Before I could ask my questions, Jerry said, "My sister called to tell me what the family's plans for the holidays were, and I couldn't take any more. I told her how much I resented doing the holiday traditions no matter how painful they were for me. I was polite. I didn't yell or curse or anything, but I kind of let her have it for asking me to do things as usual."

"What did she say?" I asked.

"Well, I feel guilty now. She started crying and *then she let me kind of have it*. She told me that if I was hurting during the holidays, it was my own fault. She said no one in the family wanted to hurt me or force me to do something that I really didn't want to do," said Jerry. "She asked me why I had never told her or the family how I felt. I didn't know what to say. So I just apologized for not telling anyone. And then she asked me how the family could help make the holidays better for me. I felt like such a jerk, but now I'm not angry with them."

Jerry had learned an important fact of life. If you need and expect help but you never ask for it, you probably will not get help. For years Jerry had mourned in angry silence about his needs and how his family and friends ignored him in his grief. If only he had asked for help that first difficult holiday season, how many days, weeks and months of anger and then resentment could he have eliminated from his grief experience? How many days, weeks and months of healing and joy did he miss because of his resentments toward others?

Jerry learned the hard way that it was best to express yourself in grief to those around you. Sharing with others can make the load of grief lighter. We mourners expect family and friends to be mind readers or psychics divining precisely what we need. We think to ourselves, "They love us and they know what we are going through. So why wouldn't they just understand and give us what we need to get through grief?"

As a counselor I am not surprised that families and friends often have communication problems. Bad or no communications are the primary causes of almost every relationship trouble. Effective communications between family members and friends can make relationships run a whole lot smoother. So it makes perfect sense that effective communications between mourners and members of their support system can make the grief process and healing for the mourner less complicated.

The specific reasons that mourners do not communicate what they are experiencing or what they need from comforters around them can vary from mourner to mourner. Generally speaking though mourners do not communicate their needs effectively for these primary reasons:

- <u>Mourners are afraid of looking weak or inferior</u>. In a culture that emphasizes independence, success and being able to pull yourself up by your own boot straps, mourners don't want to be seen as needy, inadequate and incompetent. When I meet initially with mourners in counseling sessions or support groups, I congratulate them for being brave and healthy enough to realize when they need to ask for help.

  It takes a lot of courage to share with others that you are struggling in your grief. It also takes a wise mourner concerned about his or her health and well-being to know when to ask for support and comfort. Mourners who need help, deny their pain struggle, and never seek help are the unhealthy ones in grief.

- <u>Mourners fear possible judgment or confrontation from others.</u> We mourners want others to think highly of us. Mourners often remain silent in grief to give the appearance that all is going well and that they are just fine. The price that mourners pay is that they not only grieve in silence. They will also suffer needlessly in silence.

  Have you ever had your comforters brag on how well you are doing? If they could only see what is going on inside of us, they would know that we mourners are in need of help. If we fail to let them know or see the real us with real needs, we can make our grief journey more difficult.

Other silent mourners fear that their asking for help may irritate or upset people around them. The secret for getting the help you need is to share grief thoughts, experiences and needs with safe, compassionate people and in safe places. Spend more time with safe people and less time with the unsympathetic people who have no clue or could care less what mourners are going through.

- <u>Mourners don't want to be a burden to others.</u> Our lives have up's and down's. At times in our lives, we are called upon to help, support and encourage others. Then it is our time to give. In the dark times of our lives, we need to call upon others to help support and encourage us. Then it is our turn to receive. In grief, we mourners have the opportunity and privilege to ask for and receive help from others with humility.

  Jesus gave an important principle for those who would follow His example of giving to others. In Acts 20:35 He is quoted as saying, "It is more blessed to give than to receive." When we as mourners fail to ask for help or to accept help graciously, we rob our potential comforters of the blessing of giving help to us.

- <u>Mourners want to protect others who might be mourning also.</u> Close family members and friends who share a loss can be reluctant to mourn in front of others. They fear their grief will make others sad or hurt. In many cases, the other mourners are just as reluctant to mourn openly for the same reason. The result is that no one mourns in a healthy way because everyone is avoiding the obvious. Everyone is hurting and needs to process his or her grief.

In families and friend support systems where mourning is done openly and in healthy ways, every mourner takes turn in receiving and giving support. Everyone asks for and receives the help they need to heal.

- <u>Mourners don't feel comfortable sharing what they consider to be personal business.</u> We mourners come from different family and cultural backgrounds. Therefore, we have different styles of mourning and comfort zones in sharing personal grief emotions and experiences.

  With my clients in counseling and grief support groups, I always tell them that I want them to share what they need to share and what they feel comfortable in sharing. I also emphasize that trying to go through grief alone can make their lives more complicated.

  When mourners no longer feel the pressure to "spill their guts" against their wills, they feel free to share what they are personally compelled to share. They also feel comfortable in asking for the help they realize they desperately need to lighten their grief burdens.

- <u>Mourners don't know what they need.</u> Early in grief when emotions are overwhelming, it is hard for us mourners to know what we need. Therefore, it is hard for us to know what to request from our comforters.

If we seek out supportive, sympathetic people and express our emotions to them without fear or restraint, they can know when and how to be there for us in our times of need.

DEALING WITH GRIEF DURING SPECIAL DAYS AND HOLIDAYS

Jerry's story of a lack of communication with his family about his needs and the holiday season shows another important lesson to learn about grief during special days. Once Jerry communicated his feelings and needs to his family, he and his children experienced the freedom to observe their special days and their rituals in less painful ways.

For many mourners the first year after the death of their loved one can be extremely difficult. The main cause of the difficulty is all the "firsts" the mourner observes without his or her loved one present. Those special days that are usually shared with the loved one become a painful reminder of the person's absence. The empty chair at the family table or the vacant spot around the Christmas tree as everyone opens gifts are distressing evidence that the mourner's family and life have been changed forever. During special days the mourner can experience a deeper loneliness and yearning for the presence of the loved one more than at other times.

Anticipation of the upcoming special days—an anniversary, birthday, holiday or traditional family observance—adds stress to the already stressful grief of the mourner. As a mourner you will feel pressure from others and maybe from yourself to put your grief on hold during the holidays in order not to ruin the "perfect" special days for everyone else. Don't give in to that pressure. You will only make the time more stressful for yourself.

Grief does not take a vacation or a holiday. During special days, your grief will still be present and you will still have the need to express your grief. As we have said before if you try to suppress strong emotions for any period of time, you will either emotionally explode or implode collapsing from within. In order to maintain your mental, physical, emotional, spiritual and social well-being during the holidays or special days, you need to attend to your grief needs.

Many articles and books have been written about surviving grief during the holidays focusing on the time from Thanksgiving to Christmas and New Year's Holiday. The same methods used to survive the holiday season can be used to survive any day that had special meaning for you and your loved one. By following the same principles and methods to get through Thanksgiving and Christmas you can get through birthdays, anniversary dates, Mother's and Father's Days, the Fourth of July and any other day or time period that you may be dreading.

Before we look at the survival principles for difficult days, I would like to lessen the stress you may be feeling or have felt about your first holiday season without your loved one. Certainly Thanksgiving and Christmas can be stressful and difficult to get through. In the United States lovers of the holiday season have raised the stress level of observing the "perfect holiday" to an all time, fanatical and unachievable high.

There is no such thing as a perfect holiday season except in Norman Rockwell paintings and Jimmy Stewart movies. These are idealized images that our culture has developed of what holidays and families should be. But there is no match between these idealized images and the reality of holidays and human beings. These out of touch with reality representations are similar to the idealized images of house and home we used to see on television sitcoms such as "Father Knows Best" or "Leave It to Beaver." Now did any of you have a mother who vacuumed the living room wearing pearls and high heels like Mrs. Cleaver? I didn't think so.

Here is another point on why perfect holidays are impossible. How can we expect family members and friends who often can't get along together for more than three hours at a time to act out the "perfect" holiday scenario? As long as there are people involved in the observance of the holiday season, there will be no perfect holidays. During special days and holidays, we and others are doing our best to be civil and to get along with everyone without resorting to raising our voices and unnecessary bickering.

You probably weren't expecting to have a minister and counselor tell you to lower your expectations, but that is exactly what you and everyone else need to do during the holiday season or special days in order to have a joyful, meaningful experience. Don't expect your holiday or special day without your loved one to be totally joy-filled and without any sadness or grief. It is perfectly okay to have an imperfect day, to miss your loved one and to cry if that happens.

In my grief counseling practice, I ask every client how his or her week has been between sessions. The answer from the client is almost always "Oh, it was up and down." That is the way life is...up and down... with or without grief. So then how can we as mourners expect to be up the entire holiday season when we can't make it through one week or one day without up's and down's?

During holidays and special days be realistic and expect that your days will be less than perfect and that your emotions will be changing from moment to moment. Knowing that holidays and special days are never ideal can free you from unnecessary stress. Grief is already difficult. Don't make your grief journey more difficult by having your expectations of the special days and yourself set too high.

Mourners facing approaching holiday seasons or special days in their life have taught me the importance of taking steps to be ready for those difficult times in grief. The mourner's preparation for those tough days ahead is not complicated at all. There are three simple steps for organizing yourself to survive your grief during special days.

THREE POINT PLAN FOR SURVIVING SPECIAL DAYS

- <u>Remember: the dread of the special day or time period is usually worse than experiencing the actual day.</u> This fits the principle that often we as mourners can make our grief and lives more difficult than they need to be. Our imaginations can create visions of the special day or holiday season as being much worse than it could possibly be in reality. Since mourners have a tendency to be more pessimistic than optimistic, the worry about the day can lead to needless anxiety and stress. Encourage yourself that the holiday will be better than you think even though it may be less than perfect and painful in some ways.

- <u>Make a plan for the special day. Don't just sit back and let them happen to you.</u> Mourners already feel helpless and victimized by the loss. They feel that their life is out of control. Having a plan will not actually give you control, but it can encourage you that you still have choices. The choices are in how you display your grief, how you live your life and if you will continue to be emotionally victimized by the loss.

Be flexible with your plan for the day or season. If the original plan doesn't seem to be working well, switch to Plan B. Sometimes the way to success and healing in grief or any life situation is to always remember Plan B.

• <u>Take time to remember your loved one in a special way with an activity or meaningful ritual.</u> This action meets three needs. First, you have an on-going need to remember your loved one by rituals or with behaviors that are meaningful to you. Second, this will help to fulfill your need to mourn during the special day or season. Third, you will be maintaining your spiritual and emotional relationship to the loved one. You will be actively taking the one who died and your memories of him or her into your future. Here are a few examples of rituals that you can use during the special day to remember your loved one.

• Lighting candles
• Planting a tree or starting a memorial garden.
• Creating a shadow box or memory box.
• Remembering the loved one at mealtimes or at gatherings.
• Eating a meal of the loved one's favorite foods or eating at his or her favorite restaurant.
• Wearing a physical reminder of the loved one.

- Writing letters or keeping a journal.
- Making a contribution in honor of the loved one for an organization or cause he or she would have supported.

Helpful Hints for the Special Days

In addition to having a plan for the holiday season or special days, you can help yourself and those around you by keeping the following suggestions in mind.

- **Recognize the special days or holiday season will be different. They can never be the same again.** The time your loved one was in your life, no matter how long or how brief, changed your life forever. He or she has helped make you who you are.

   Part of the change resulting from the death is no longer being able to share events such as special days with them. Understanding this change and knowing that other changes will take place in your life is part of accepting your new reality, adapting to the changes and moving toward healing. In the meantime, you can maintain your changed relationship with the loved one by remembering them, honoring what they have given you by passing it on to others and living your life well.

- **Do only what gives you comfort and is meaningful.** Make a list of the usual activities you do on the special day. If the activities are too painful for you at this time, eliminate them from the list. In time you may want to return to these activities or replace them with new activities.

- **Remember crying or expressing your grief openly will not ruin the holidays or special days for you or anyone else.** For your own well-being, mourn with people who make you feel comfortable and in places that make you feel safe. When you mourn, compassionate family members and friends will understand. Your mourning also gives them the opportunity to be there for you with support and comfort. Accept their help graciously. Teach them what you need.

- **Talk with your family and friends about how you will observe the time.** Jerry learned the importance of communicating his grief needs to family members. If you don't feel up to doing all the planned activities for the day, let others know at what level you will or will not be participating. Example: You may want to stay only through dinner and the opening of gifts at Christmas rather than spending the whole day with the family.

- **Make new meaningful traditions.** Some family members or friends may protest your changing your activities by saying that it won't be right if you don't follow the traditions of the past. Let them know that you can do things differently and it will not change the meaning for you or anyone else. Next year you may decide to return to the traditions of the special day or replace the traditions with new ones.

  Do you know how traditions start? Someone decides that a certain activity or ritual will be a fit and meaningful way to celebrate or honor a special occasion. Then when they do it a second time, the activity becomes a tradition. Traditions are simply rituals that reinforce our values and beliefs in meaningful ways. When those traditional activities are no longer meaningful, the ritual can be replaced with an equally meaningful new ritual.

- **Be prepared for grief outbursts and don't avoid them.** Before families or friends get together, you may want to have some time to mourn alone. When I know that I might have a grief outburst at a family activity, I get out the family album and look at pictures before the gathering. This gives me some time to mourn in private and to vent grief emotions prior to the special day. This planned grieving session doesn't guarantee that I won't still have a grief outburst on the special day. If I do, I know that crying will not ruin the day for me or anyone else.

- **Be kind to yourself and accept help from others.** Don't set your expectations too high for yourself or the special day. If at any time you need help from others, let them know.

- **Take care of yourself and don't overdo.** Special days and celebrations can be a time of lots of activities. Don't overdo. Have fun, but watch your food and alcohol consumption. Overdoing can add emotional and physical stress to your already stressed mind and body.

- **Remember why you are observing this special time.** Holidays and special days are observed for usually two reasons. First, the observation of the day reinforces your values and your belief system. In other words, this day has a special meaning to you. Second, you are gathering together with others to share the importance of the day and to enjoy each others' company.

Although your loved one is no longer physically there to share the time with you, you can still share the special day with them by remembering and honoring his or her life in meaningful, comforting activities. Remember to not expect or try to force others to mourn or remember the person in the same way that you do if they do not want to.

On these special days you, your family and friends will be making memories for the future. A good question to ask yourself in how you cope with your grief and the special day is "How do I want to be remembered?"

- **Remember that you will get through these difficult days.** Although the special day may be difficult, you have the choice on how to observe it. You are making an active choice on how you will deal with the special day and your grief. You have chosen not to be continually victimized emotionally by your grief.

Your Rights As A Mourner on Special Days

Mourners are shamed sometimes into thinking that they are being selfish if they consider their needs in how they observe these days. Certainly the holiday season and other special days should be a time when the individual's focus is on considerations of others. Keep in mind though that in order to be able to reach out to others during holidays that you as a mourner still have to exercise self care surrounding your emotional wounds of grief. This self care includes remembering your rights as a mourner on special days.

- <u>You have a right to say "time out."</u>
    When situations or activities become painful and overwhelming for you, you have the right to excuse yourself and take care of your personal grief needs. Friends and family members may not always be considerate of these needs. You are the expert on your grief and you have the ability to determine your limitations on special days. Communicate your needs and take care of yourself without shame or guilt.

- <u>You have a right to be honest and kind.</u>
    When you do communicate your needs to others, do so with patience and without intentionally hurting others' feelings.

- <u>You have a right to do things differently.</u>
    Just because you have always observed special days with specific traditions doesn't mean you can't change activities or the schedule. Changing how you do the special day will not ruin it for you or anyone else.

- <u>You have a right to be where you want to be.</u>
    Be in places that you feel safe to mourn if a grief outburst should happen. Be with people who make you feel comfortable and supported.

- <u>You have a right to enjoy yourself and have fun.</u>
  Those mourning the loss of a loved one can still enjoy the activities of special days. This means that you can not only choose activities that honor your loved one in meaningful ways but that you can also choose activities that are just fun.

- <u>You have a right to be flexible in your plans.</u> If your plan for the day falls apart or doesn't work for you, be willing to change to another plan or set of activities.

- <u>You have a right to rest, peace and solitude. You don't have to be constantly busy or active.</u> Grief is hard work and it can drain all your energy physically, emotionally and spiritually. Take time to rest and save your energy for important activities.

- <u>You have a right to do it all different again next year. In other words, you have a right to change your mind.</u> Grief changes and your needs as a mourner will change over time. You may feel the need to change activities as time passes in your grief. Mourners can often return to the old traditions observing special days as the intense pain of early grief changes or diminishes.

- <u>You have a right to an occasional bad moment or day.</u> Sometimes it is healthy to feel sad, depressed, angry or guilty. In grief these emotions happen to us without our choice. We as mourners still have a choice though in the behavior we choose to express grief emotions. Bad days or moments usually pass. You can survive them. As time passes these occurrences of bad times in your grief can become fewer and fewer and farther and farther apart.

Caring for Grieving Children on Special Days

Mourning children and teens are affected by special days also. They need the support and comfort of others just as much as their parents and other adult family members do. Often though they are overlooked mourners because adults are occupied with or overwhelmed by their own grief.

If children or teens are sharing your grief experience, you can reach out to them also to provide them compassionate support, reassurance and opportunities to express their grief emotions.

- Include children & teens in the special day planning. Make young people a part of the decision-making process in choosing the activities for the special day. Children appreciate that adults consider their feelings and opinions when making plans.

- Prepare children for any changes in routine. Children need order and schedule in their lives in order to feel secure. Unexpected changes can raise the anxiety and stress levels for children and teens. When children feel forced to do things differently from what has always been done, they may resort to protest and acting out behavior.

- Give children added comfort and reassurance. The number one need of mourning children is security. They want to know that they are safe and cared for. Be patient and take time to answer their constant questions about who will be doing what and what will happen next.

- <u>Give children some slack or grace on their behavior, but enforce important rules or bound-aries.</u> Most children and teens under stressful situations will act out or display inappropriate or unusual behavior. Often it is hard for stressed out, mourning adults to remember this fact. Let the child or teen feel your support and love, but at the same time enforce necessary rules and boundaries when they act out.

- <u>Let children know that they can talk openly about their feelings and fears.</u> Make children and teens feel safe to talk about their concerns and needs in their grief. Children who do not feel supported during times of crisis will develop coping skills that will help them survive but may not be healthy coping skills. As adults it is our duty to be role models for children of what healthy adults do in bad stressful situations.

REMEMBER: For adults and children facing the challenges of upcoming special days and holidays in grief, the key to successfully navigating those times is three-fold:

1. Keep in mind that the dread of the holiday or special day usually is worse than going through the day itself. Make sure that you will have your support system or supportive people available on that day if your grief becomes overwhelming.

2. Develop a plan for the holiday or special day. Don't let the day and all that comes with it just happen to you. Also be flexible with your plan. If your first plan isn't working, you might have to resort to Plan B.
3. Remember and honor your loved one who has died in a meaningful way on that day. Your grief can not be put on hold. If you have a grief outburst, you will not ruin the day for yourself or anyone else.

Share each other's burdens, and in this way obey the law of Christ. (Galatians 6:2 NLV)

CHAPTER EIGHT

WHEN WELL-INTENTIONED PEOPLE GO WRONG

…... mourners can be difficult to help. Mourners are on edge most of the time. They can react negatively to almost any statement or behavior. Comforters can become paralyzed by the fear of saying the wrong thing. People supporting mourners don't want to inflict more pain and trauma.

Sunday morning in church. A few years after the accident.

I n church we referred to it as "Hug and Howdy Time." After the pulpit announcements, the congregation members were encouraged to greet the people sitting around them. It was a time to welcome visitors and a chance to visit with fellow church members.

This Sunday at Hug and Howdy Time, a smiling lady in the pew in front of us turned to my daughter Sarah and me. "Hi, I'm Jamie Jones," she said as she extended her hand to me. "I just placed membership a few months ago. I moved here from Little Rock."

"Hi, Jamie. Welcome to the church," I said as I smiled back to her and shook her hand. "I'm Larry Barber, and this is my....."

"Barber? Barber!" she said as she digested my last name. "Barber. Do I know your wife?"

Oh, no! I did not want to go there now. Not this morning during church. Not in this friendly conversation with a stranger in front of my daughter. I also wanted to spare Jamie any embarrassment for not knowing that my wife Cindy was dead. I stalled trying to think of the best way to back out of this awkward conversation. The only statement I could come up with under the pressure of the moment was to say, "You probably do."

"So is she here this morning?" asked Jamie still shaking my hand.

"No, Jamie," I said still smiling while slowly and deliberately retrieving my hand. "She's not here."

"Oh," said Jamie with a concerned look coming over her face. "Is she sick?"

"No," I replied while praying that Jamie would let go of this line of questioning and end the conversation. "She's not sick."

"Is she out of town?" Jamie went further in her pursuit of knowledge.

"Yes," I smiled. "My wife is out of town." Sarah cleared her throat and looked at me. My quick look to Sarah in response was silently saying, "Well, I'm not lying. She is out town! Sort of."

"Is she visiting relatives?" Jamie said as she leaned forward to receive my answer. Obviously this woman was not going to quit.

"Yes, she is with relatives," I sighed. "Visiting with relatives."

"And where do they live?" asked Jamie the interrogator.

129

I looked to Sarah. She shrugged. I turned to Jamie. My patience was wearing thin. "Heaven. They live in heaven," I said with as much politeness as I could muster. "My wife is dead and she is with relatives in Heaven."

The color drained from Jamie's face. "Oh, I am so sorry. I didn't know. I am so…."

I told Jamie that it was all right <u>because she did not know</u>. At that moment church resumed and we all sat into our places. My feelings of irritation and awkwardness caused by my conversation with Jamie soon faded as Sarah and I became immersed in the worship service.

But the embarrassment and awkwardness of the moment obviously did not fade for Jamie. I can only guess that she brooded over the incident throughout the entire church service. When the "Amen" of the closing prayer was said, Jamie turned to me again intent on bringing our conversation to a positive ending for her.

Dressed that day in jeans and a t-shirt, my usually patient daughter Sarah looked angry with the situation and ready to bolt for home. Jamie continued, "I am really sorry. I just was trying to be…."

"I know. I know," I said trying not to show my frustration. "I told you it's okay."

"Yes, but what I said probably caused you pain," she said looking over at Sarah. "And I said it in front of your son…." By the way, did I mention Sarah wore her hair short? And my son Christian was not anywhere near us?

My efforts at being polite and protecting Jamie from the truth were suddenly over. "Sarah is my DAUGHTER," I said slowly.

Again all the color drained from Jamie's face. She had stuck both feet in her mouth, and she realized it. She excused herself and quickly disappeared. I never saw Jamie again. I imagine she spent much of her time avoiding Sarah and me if she spotted us at church.

Jamie taught me an important lesson that day. Even well meaning people are going to say things that cause mourners awkward moments, struggles in grief, and sometimes even pain. To this day I don't hold any anger or ill will toward Jamie. I can forgive Jamie for the uncomfortable moments she caused Sarah and me because I know that she just didn't know. She was trying to be friendly, and she didn't have a clue.

I am sharing the story of my conversation with Jamie for two reasons. One, I want mourners to know that there will be difficult, awkward and sometimes painful things said and done to them by others. Under the stress of grief and pain, mourners may be tempted to be brutally honest and blunt in their responses to these statements. In fact, your first thought may be to strike out to cause as much pain for the potential comforter as they have inflicted on you. You may even want to use them as the target of the built up anger you have been saving for weeks.

Mourners are never justified in hurting others simply because they hurt. The majority of comforters want to ease your grief pain, not inflict more pain. The reason they say the wrong things is not that they are mean or stupid. The reason they say these wrong things is that they have no clue what we need to hear as mourners.

Your response to those who say the wrong things for the right reasons is to consider first their hearts and second their feelings. As mourners our reactions to those who have no clue should be a well thought out reply showing understanding for their lack of knowledge or skills to comfort well. As mourners, we can educate comforters about our grief and what we need. Extending patience and forgiveness to these comforters will ease your grief process.

What about those who **are** mean spirited and want to complicate our lives as mourners? The best response to difficult people is to spend only the time necessary with them. When you are with difficult people who complicate your grief intentionally, you do have the right to defend your healthy mourning. You still will not be justified though in simply hurting them because you are hurting. Going for the jugular in response to someone who has hurt you can cause further complications in the relationship and in your grief journey.

The second reason I have shared Jamie's story is that I want comforters to know that their words to mourners should be considered carefully before spoken. We all say things unintentionally that make others uncomfortable or experience emotional pain. Jamie's problem was that she kept saying more wrong things in an effort to correct the situation and make herself feel better. Her focus was not on the mourners' needs, but on her own. Comforters, when your primary focus in a conversation with a mourner becomes you and not the mourner, you have become an ineffective comforter.

Once you realize that you have said something that causes a mourner to be in pain or uncomfortable, please apologize immediately and wait for the mourner to direct the conversation further. Jamie did not know when to be silent or quit trying to make herself feel better. Let the mourner educate you about what they want to talk about and what they need from you as a comforter.

As a mourner and bereavement counselor I know that mourners can be difficult to help. Mourners are on edge most of the time. They can react negatively to almost any statement or behavior. Comforters can become paralyzed by the fear of saying the wrong thing. People supporting mourners don't want to inflict more pain and trauma.

Let me take the pressure off of you comforters. What is important to the mourner is not what you say or do. What is important to us mourners is that you are physically, mentally, emotionally and spiritually present for us. We just want to know you sincerely care and are available when we need help.

Now, mourners and comforters, I am including a list of suggested ways that comforters can be most helpful to mourners. Those in grief can use this list to educate their support system members. Don't beat comforters over the head with suggestions on this list simply to point out how clueless they are. Use the list in a patient, understanding and loving way to show your comforters how they can meet your needs.

Mourners, remember too that there may come a time when you can reach out to others mourners to help them. Keep this list nearby to remind you of what they need to help, support and encourage them. Use your grief experience to reach out to other mourners with compassion, empathy and kindness.

Potential comforters can use this list of suggestions to develop skills and methods to better address the needs of mourners. When you as potential comforters forget your fear of saying or doing the wrong thing and just do something out of your compassion, you can have confidence in reaching out to ease someone's grief struggle.

SUGGESTIONS FOR THOSE HELPING PEOPLE IN GRIEF

Compiled by Real Life, Experienced Mourners
In Grief Support Groups

- <u>Be aware of the person's loss and emotional state.</u>

    In order to be aware of a person's grief situation, a comforter must be involved with the people around him or her. At home, at the workplace, at church and in the community the potential comforter has to be sincerely concerned with and active in other peoples' lives.

- <u>Be present when the mourner needs you.</u>

    This is practicing the ministry of presence, being there for the mourner by being available to provide support, comfort and encouragement. Don't hover or force yourself on the person. When help is offered, it should be when the mourner asks or gives permission for you to take action on their behalf and for their well being.

    Remember the mourner does not need to be fixed or to have his or her problems solved. Be prepared to listen and not judge what the mourner shares with you. You are there to walk with them through this journey, not guide them. Also let them do most of the talking. In the pain of grief, the mourner will most likely not be able to hear and appreciate the comfort or wisdom you might feel compelled to share with them. Above all, avoid giving unsolicited advice.

- <u>Be active in helping the person in grief.</u>

The best support you can provide a mourner is to honor their story, experiences and thoughts they share at the moment. Sometimes what mourners reveal can be painful, uncomfortable or grisly. They need to tell their story though. Just be patient and listen.

Listen and reflect their feelings back to them. Mourners need to express themselves and to be affirmed. All people, especially those in grief, have two great needs. First, they want to be able to express themselves without fear of judgment or critiques. Second, they want to know that they have been heard and understood. Reflecting back what the mourner has told you, will meet the mourners' communications needs and help them to move toward healing.

Don't tell mourners "If you need anything, just call me." Put yourselves in their shoes and do for them what you might want others to do for you. And do it without asking permission. If you ask permission, nine times out of ten the mourner will decline the offer because they don't want to be a burden.

You can do such comforting deeds as cleaning their home, helping them with their shopping, or babysitting their children to give them a night out. Remember, mourners appreciate more what you do to show you sincerely care rather than what you say.

After the deaths of my wife and daughter, one gentleman offered to mow my yard. At first I protested. I was a strong man, not some helpless widower. Then I saw the sincere care and need to help my family in his offer. You know,

I got used to watching him mow my yard over the next few months. I looked forward to visiting with him each time he showed up with his lawn-mower. I watched through tears from my window as he showed how much my friendship and my family meant to him.

- <u>Don't avoid the person or act as if nothing happened.</u> One of the most disappointing experiences for mourners can be to have people who they counted on for support suddenly disappear from their lives. Don't use the excuses "I wouldn't know what to say or do" or "I don't want to intrude in their lives right now" to do nothing for the mourner.

- <u>Don't stop or cut short the person's grief process.</u> Let the mourner cry or express their grief emotions. Don't say things like "Oh, you know (your loved one) wouldn't want you to be sad."

  When the mourner starts to cry, <u>let them reach for the tissue</u>. Don't immediately hand it to them. The well intentioned offer of a tissue can shut down the expression of sadness before the mourner completes his or her grief outburst.

- <u>Don't try to orchestrate the person's grief process.</u> Avoid giving unsolicited advice or direction for what the mourner should or should not do in their grief. Don't immediately prescribe for them the actions or coping skills that you or other mourners have used in the past. Remember, each person's grief is unique. The mourner needs to choose the options in mourning that will work well for him or her.

- <u>Don't judge the person or his or her circum-stance.</u> Avoid telling the mourner why the death or situations leading up to the death took place. Steer clear of telling the mourner that "Everything will be all right" or that "Everything happens for a reason." There may be truth in those state-ments, but they are not comforting statements for mourners missing their loved one. The mourner does not want to think others are saying or even implying that the death of a loved one will be a temporary setback that can soon be forgotten.

- <u>Don't pontificate on the theological ramifications of the tragedy or the resulting grief.</u> (I put this rule in for ministers, chaplains and well-meaning church members.) Don't try to make the situation better by explaining it in spiritual or theological terms.

  One person told me that my losses happened because God was trying to teach me something. I immediately thought that if I needed a lesson from God then I was at fault for the deaths of my wife Cindy and my daughter Katie. I didn't need to have this comforter make me feel any more guilt than I already did.

- <u>Don't belittle or discount their feelings.</u> Stay away from statements like "You shouldn't feel that way." Listen to the mourner's feelings and don't judge their validity. Let them feel what they feel at the moment. A more appropriate response might be to affirm the person's feelings by saying "I could see how you might feel that way."

- <u>Don't say "I know how you feel."</u> This statement is one quick way to get a rise out of an angry mourner or to shut down him or her from any further expression of grief emotions.

- <u>Don't say "I am praying for you" when you aren't.</u> Often this declaration is made at the end of a conversation with the mourner as a way for the comforter to exit to other activities. The comforter may have every intention of praying for the person, but they might forget to do so later.

  When I tell someone that I will pray for them, I do it right then and there. I shoot a short "arrow" prayer straight up to God. That keeps me from forgetting my promise to pray.

- <u>Never use "at least" statements.</u> Some of the most discomforting statements made to mourners start with the words "At least." Steer clear of such statements as:

  At least you have other children....or you can still have other children.

  At least you had (however many) good years of marriage together....

  At least they didn't suffer....

  At least you know they are in a better place....

  At least you're young. You can always remarry....

- <u>Think before you speak.</u> After over twelve years of working with grieving people, I have collected some of the most common statements made by would-be comforters that deeply upset the mourner. Please avoid these hurtful clichés.

Waxing theological:
It's God will....
God needed him (her) more than we did...
God never gives you more than you can handle...
He (She) is in a better place....
She (He) is an angel now looking over you....
Remember, God is in control....

Waxing philosophical:
Everything happens for a reason...
People die every day. It's just part of life....
It was his (her) time...
It's all for the best....
It will get better...or...It will be all right...

Unwelcome advice:
You just need to move on....
It won't help to dwell on the past (or the death)...
You need to get busy and just forget....
Aren't you going to go back to work? Get your mind off the loss...
I could introduce you to someone nice. I don't want you to be alone...
Are you able to have another baby?
Quit throwing your pity party! It's been three months....
You need to get rid of all of his (her) stuff...(And when you do, can I have the....?)

The most perplexing statement made by comforters for me and many other mourners is to be
told how well we are doing. Usually the statements
take the form of something such as "You are so
strong and doing so well. I don't know how you do
it." Mourners hear this compliment and think, "Do

I have any other choice? What do you want me to do? Fall apart before your eyes? Believe me, inside I am falling apart."

What should the grief comforter do? Keep your responses to mourners simple, heartfelt and sincere:

Give the mourner a hug, but ask if they mind a hug first.

Tell the mourner you love him (her), care for him (her) and feel sad about the death and how it has changed his (her) life.

Send a card with a short, down-to-earth message. The most touching card I received was from a minister who said, "I cannot even imagine the unspeakable pain you must be going through." He didn't have to say anything else.

- If you think that you are about to say something that will be inspirational, profound and life-changing to the mourner, please just keep your mouth shut and save it for later. The mourner is in so much pain and distress that they cannot hear the comfort in even the most truthful spiritual or philosophical statements. Often comforters are hoping for a quick fix of the mourner with just a few wisely chosen words uttered by them. In other words, these comforters are really saying these words to make themselves feel or look good.

- **Don't let your fear of doing or saying the wrong thing to a mourner keep you from doing anything at all.** In comforting those in grief, you need to adopt the oath of physicians and counselors to do no harm to the person you are trying to support. Chances are that you will occasionally say or do something that is not very comforting, but doing or saying something is better than abandoning the mourner all together.

Mourners want to know that you and others do care for them by being present, by listening without judgment or advice, and by showing how much you care for them. When a mourner knows that a comforter truly cares about her (him), the mourner can forgive an occasional verbal or behavioral mistake.

May our Lord Jesus Christ himself and God our Father, who has loved us and given us everlasting comfort and hope which we don't deserve, comfort your hearts with all comfort, and help you in every good thing you say and do. (2 Thessalonians 2:16-17 NIV)

NOTE TO READER: When someone asks me as a mourner how I am doing, what should I say? Do I tell them the truth or what I think they want to hear? There is no one answer for all mourners and all situations to this question. For most mourners, they are reluctant to tell others how they are really doing. So they usually answer with the standard "Fine."

I tell clients and grief group members to share honestly only in places and with people who make them safe. Most mourners can tell if the person is sincere in wanting to know how they are really doing or just saying "How are you?" as a casual greeting. If the person really is sincere and they make you feel safe, let them know how you are doing. How you describe your well being is up to you.

If you feel the person asking how you are is not really interested, say diplomatically and graciously what you want. Here are some of the responses most commonly shared by mourners with me:

- I'm doing okay.
- I've done better, but I'll be fine.
- I'm doing the best I can.
- Oh, fair to middlin'.
- So so. And you?
- If you really want to know, I can tell you.

CHAPTER NINE

YOU FEEL WHAT YOU FEEL

Everyone's grief is complicated by the distinctive details and situations surrounding the unique, one-of-a-kind in the all the universe relationship we have with the loved one. Each of these unique complications of our grief results in emotions that can be troubling and scary to the mourner.

In a session of a grief support group meeting in Fort Worth, Texas.

"I just don't understand all this talk about people being angry after their loved one dies," said Olivia, a prim and proper English widow. Her face changed from its usually cheery appearance to one deep in thought as she continued in that cultured English accent that everyone in the group loved to hear each session. "I've never been angry since Charles died. I have no reason to be angry."

Olivia had married her "Yank" boyfriend Charles while he was stationed near London during World War II. Charles had died after months of chemotherapy and time spent in hospice care.

"I could never be angry with Charles. It wasn't his fault that he got cancer and died. Poor thing. Never smoked or drank a day in his life," sighed Olivia. A tear rolled down her cheek. "I couldn't be angry at the doctors or the hospital or hospice. They gave Charles the best treatment possible. Lovely people."

"And what's the use of being angry at God or life?" asked Olivia as her eyes moved across all the sympathetic faces looking back at her. "We all die, right? It's not like we expect people to live forever. So, I just don't understand how people can waste their time being angry over something that you can't blame anyone for causing. Life and death go together. I have never been angry about my loss."

This was the fifth time Olivia had given this speech in five sessions. I leaned toward Olivia and replied, "Well, every person who grieves is different. No one said you have to be angry. There is no one right way to get through grief. It sounds like you and everyone around Charles did your best for him."

"Yes, we did," said Olivia in almost a whisper as her head dropped. Then she looked back up at me. "Terrible waste of time being angry. It wouldn't be right. There's no reason to be angry."

I nodded and asked, "Olivia, let's talk about some other feelings. Do you ever feel frustrated?"

"Of course," she replied. "There are so many things every day to be frustrated over. Taking care of paperwork, paying our bills to everyone who provided medical treatment for Charles, talking to Social Security....." Olivia's voice trailed off.

"And do you ever feel irritated?" I asked.

"Oh yes, definitely," replied Olivia. "I am so on edge all the time that it doesn't take much to get me going." Olivia fell into silence. "I see where you are going. I guess that I am a bit....upset. I am upset that Charles died and upset at all this stuff I have to put up with."

"Yes, I can see why you would be...uh..upset," I said. "And, Olivia, it's okay to be upset."

"Yes, I guess I have been upset. And frustrated and irritated," declared Olivia "But that doesn't mean I am angry! Being angry would be silly." Everyone in the group including Olivia laughed.

Grief is filled with uncomfortable, unpleasant and often painful emotions. For Olivia, anger was a feeling to be avoided and denied because it was also an emotion that did not make sense to her. Many emotions we mourners have don't make sense to us and are threatening to our need to feel secure and in control. Remember, in grief we mourners do not choose the emotions we experience. The feelings just seem to happen. They are neither good nor bad. They just exist to help us process our loss.

Anger is probably the second most common emotion experienced by mourners. I would guess number one would be sadness, of course. Our culture sometimes paints anger as negative, destructive and inappropriate. But anger is very simply not liking how things are and wanting things to be different. Therefore, anger can be seen as a very justifiable feeling for a mourner who does not want to be forced to live without the physical presence of a dear loved one.

Also anger has many shades or levels. Olivia may have thought of anger in grief as being the raging wrath of an out of control mourner. That's just one form of anger. On the opposite end of the anger spectrum is irritation and frustration. You might call those two feelings Anger Light.

Very rarely is anger the primary emotion being felt by a person expressing it. Anger is often secondary and a cover up emotion for what people are initially feeling in a life event or situation. Anger can be the visible, displayed emotion keeping fear and the feeling of being threatened hidden from public view.

Whether Olivia ever admitted that she was experiencing anger in her constant battle with the irritations and frustrations of life after loss, she did have a turning point in her grief journey. She learned that whatever emotion resulted from her loss and its consequences that those experienced emotions were natural. She could not choose how she felt, but she could choose how she responded to her often uncomfortable grief emotions.

Mourners need to remember that grief emotions are simply what we feel in the human experience of loss after the death of a loved one. We feel what we feel. The feeling and thoughts we have are not bad in and of themselves. What we do with these grief emotions and experiences in the behavior we choose are either good or bad, appropriate or inappropriate, healthy or unhealthy, or constructive or destructive.

As humans we have many emotions and thoughts that make us feel uncomfortable. Think about that person at work that is difficult to work with. Haven't you some days thought that if he or she said just one more word to you that you would knock them up against the wall? Of course, you didn't. You felt an unpleasant emotion, anger, and you thought about an action that you decided would result in inappropriate behavior on your part as a co-worker. You chose wisely. You can also choose wisely on how you respond to your grief emotions and thoughts.

Mourners can help themselves to confront these painful, uncomfortable emotions and thoughts by understanding the answers to some very important questions about grief emotions.

Can We Escape the Emotions of Grief? <u>NO!</u>

We can suppress, deny, stifle, avoid and run from our thoughts and emotions during grief. But these measures are only temporary escapes from the emotions that are the natural result of the impact of loss on our lives. Grief emotions help us to turn inward at a time when reflection and review help us to cope with major changes in our life and relationships.

Death has changed us forever and the expression of grief emotions over the loss of a valuable person will take place—with or without our permission. Feelings or thoughts denied or avoided will find expression in our lives sooner or later. Acknowledging and using our thoughts and grief emotions to process what has taken place will relieve the stress of grief, move us toward healing and help us to put our loss in context.

Can We Control the Emotions of Grief? <u>NO!</u>

How can we not feel sad, depressed, angry and the many other grief emotions concerning the loss of our valued loved one? Grief and its emotions can motivate us to live in a way that honors and celebrates the life of our loved one.

Many of us fear losing control if we allow ourselves to express the emotions of grief. Expressing these emotions in constructive ways releases us to process our grief. Many of us also fear the discomfort of expressing emotions. Expressing grief emotions in constructive ways brings relief and helps us heal. Many of us fear being embarrassed in front of others by honestly expressing our emotions. Expressing your grief emotions in constructive ways to others gives them an opportunity to support and comfort us.

Do We Have to Become Slaves to the Emotions of Grief? <u>NO!</u>

We can't control our emotions, but at the same time, our emotions do not have to control our behavior. We have a choice as to how we respond. The key is to acknowledge and address emotions in ways that are beneficial to us and to those who are trying to help us through grief.

When Do Emotions Keep Me From Healing?

When thoughts or emotions preoccupy us so much that we are distracted from processing grief, we become stuck in our grief. These obsessions with emotions and thoughts (including the details of our loss, our unfinished business or unresolved differences with the loved one) keep us from mourning in a healthy way. Guilt, anger and resentment result – causing us to focus on other things than the grief process that can help us heal.

Are you the type of person who can remember a wrong done to you and feel just as angry or betrayed as you did when it happened? That's an example of what can happen to the mourner who becomes fixated on a specific event or detail about the death. The mourner becomes obsessed exclusively with the irritating factor. The result is that the mourner never fully processes the event so that he or she can move forward in grief.

What Can I Do With the Emotions of Grief That Keep Me From Healing?

Although grief emotions cannot be chosen, each emotion experienced can be evaluated. We mourners need to ask ourselves why we feel what we do. Where do these emotions come from? Often these emotions are the result of beliefs or expectations we have of life, of others and us.

These beliefs or expectations can be realistic or unrealistic, logical or illogical. Unrealistic expectations or illogical beliefs (such as "My life must always be pleasurable," or "My relationships must always be perfect," or "Other people should always treat me fairly.") only set us up for failure. Often these illogical beliefs and unrealistic expectations are the results of coping skills or beliefs we developed early in life.

These unrealistic expectations and illogical beliefs keep us from moving through life and through grief in a healthy way. The faulty expectations or beliefs behind an emotion or thought need to be evaluated and replaced with more logical, realistic beliefs. Once these unrealistic expectations or illogical beliefs are tossed, the destructive emotions and behavior that come with them can disappear. We have a choice on how we respond to life situations and crises.

Grief is a stress reaction that affects us physically, mentally, spiritually, emotionally and even socially. Everyone's grief is complicated by the distinctive details and situations surrounding the unique, one-of-a-kind in the all the universe relationship we have with the loved one. Each of these unique complications of our grief results in emotions that can be troubling and scary to the mourner.

The most important thing to realize is that your reactions in grief are natural for you. That is, if you are experiencing these strange emotions, progressing in grief, and doing no damage to yourself or those around you, then it is natural.

<u>How do you know that you are dealing with your grief emotions in a beneficial way?</u> Some key components to healthy grieving include:

- **Acknowledging the many and varied emotions connected with grief**
  Painful or uncomfortable emotions can make mourners feel out of control and irrational. These emotions are less threatening when the mourner remembers that he or she does have a choice on how to react to an emotion.

- **Finding appropriate ways to express these emotions in constructive ways rather than in destructive ways that hurt you or others**
  Even the emotions that we mourners label as "negative" can be motivators for us to take action that help us to process our grief, to heal and to be able to ask those around us for help and support.

  For example, the founder of the organization Mothers Against Drunk Drivers (MADD) used the emotion of anger to wage what is now a nationwide campaign against drunk driving. The so called "negative" emotion of anger was turned into a positive, constructive force for change and the saving of lives on the highways.

- **Searching for ways to resolve or be at peace with issues of emotional chaos**

  Mourners need to examine their feelings of guilt, anger and regret to determine if they are real or imagined, justified or illogical. These feelings prod and motivate the mourner to fully evaluate their loss and its impact. These feelings often indicate areas the mourner can focus on and sort out to move toward healing.

- **Looking for ways to remember the good and still acknowledge the humanity of the person**
  Our culture tells us to honor the dead and to never speak ill of them. We mourners also tend to almost deify the person who died in our selective memories concerning them. But no person, including your loved ones or mine, are perfect. Our loved ones possessed wonderful traits and not so wonderful traits.
  Try to be as honest in your memories of your loved one to reflect him or her as they really were in life. Maybe they were not the perfect spouse, parent, child, family member or friend that we wanted them to be. Forgive them for the times they upset you or disappointed you. Remember, you will want your loved ones to be just as forgiving of you after you die.

- **Seeking to honor and remember your loved one**
  One-time funerals and memorials after a death do not bring "closure" or finality to your relationship or your loss. As long as you love and miss this significant person, you have a need to memorialize them on a regular basis. Try to honor and remember your loved one in suitable, meaningful ways throughout your grief.

- **Turning toward hopefulness and gratitude for the life of your loved one**
  As the mourner progress in grief, the focus on emotions and thoughts about the death will change.

At the beginning of grief, the mourner concentrates on the death, the factors surrounding the loss and what the mourner will never have again. As time passes, the focus of the mourner can be redirected to how the loved one lived and the people she or he influenced.

With that change of focus, the mourner can center on what gifts the loved one shared with him or her that can never be taken away. A person's life is not defined by how the person dies, but in the type of life lived and the life's influence on others.

Although every mourner's grief is unique, there are some commonalities that the mourner can use to prepare for the grief journey. Below are some common emotions that can be troubling or scary for mourners. Keep in mind that you personally may not experience all of these emotions. You may even be able to add a few emotions to your list that are not here.

Knowing what possibly lies ahead in your grief can help lighten your load. Here are some of the common experiences and struggles of other mourners in their grief journey.

Common Troubling Emotions Experienced During Grief

- **Shock, denial, numbness and disbelief**
  This is the only truly predictable part of grief—the emotional numbness that comes at the beginning of the grief journey. In this shock phase your body and mind only allow you to accept as much of the new reality as you can at the moment. As time passes you will begin your work of accepting the loss fully.

- **Disorganization, confusion, searching, yearning**
  Your life has been shattered by the death of your loved one. These emotions arise from your need to pick up the pieces and to put your life and yourself back together. In order for there to be a re-organization of your life later, there must be disorganization. This allows you as a mourner to review the situation and to refocus and reframe the loss and your future life without the person physically present.

- **Anxiety, panic, fear, abandonment**
  These emotions result from your loss of security and a sudden feeling of being very much alone. When someone you love dies, this world suddenly seems an unsafe and threatening place in which to live.

  Vivian and her husband Bob had been married for almost fifty years when Bob died of a heart attack. Vivian shared with her grief support group that she had become extremely anxious and fearful at nights in her home. She was constantly checking the locks on the doors and windows to make sure no one could get in. Every little noise made her jump.

  "It was so different in the house when Bob was still alive, said Vivian. "I always knew he was there. Even when he was in the living room watching sports and I was in the other end of the house working on my crafts, I felt comfortable and safe. Just knowing he was in the house made me feel protected."

  After a death, the world becomes a scary place. We become more aware of just how vulnerable we are without our loved one. We also come to the harsh realization that Death is a certainty for everyone of us. Therefore, we begin to focus on the possible deaths of other loved ones in our life.

As author and scholar C.S. Lewis described his feelings after the death of his wife, *"No one ever told me that grief felt so like fear."* (Lewis, 1961. *A Grief Observed,* Faber and Faber Limited, London)

- **Explosive emotions (Emotions that can cause a feeling of being out of control)**
Anger and anxiety are among the common grief emotions which can become overwhelming and cause us to feel totally helpless and hopeless. If the mourner reacts continuously with explosive, uncontrollable emotions in his or her grief, professional help may be needed.

- **Guilt, regret, self-reproach**
You begin to ask "what if" questions about your perceived or real involvement in the person's life and the loss itself. Are you or someone else to blame? Could you have stop or prevented the death from taking place? Guilt is a common expression of grief. Guilt can come in many forms:

- **Survival guilt**:
We question why our loved one died and we are still here. We question whether we or others deserved to die more than our loved one did. It is common to hear mourners say, "It should have been me that died instead of them."

- **Long-standing personality trait**:
  Some mourners already have a personality that causes them to feel guilty when anything goes wrong. In grief, we often feel as if we are being punished. We wonder what we did wrong and how we can make amends.

- **Joy-Guilt**:
  This type of guilt is felt immediately after the mourner experiences joy or pleasure during his or her grief. Mourners feel that their "positive" emotions are inappropriate in a life without the loved one present. They feel that their joy or pleasure is a betrayal to the one who died. The mourner often equates moving on in the grief journey with forgetting or abandoning the loved one.

- **Magical Thinking Guilt**:
  This guilt results when a mourner feels strongly that they caused the death by something that they did or did not do. This feeling is common in young mourners, especially children, who are not able to see cause and effect as mature adults do. For example children may think that they could have stopped their mother's heart attack by being a better son or daughter and not causing their mother stress.

  Adults can also display magical thinking guilt. One member of a grief support group I facilitated stated one night that he had killed his wife of eighteen years. When I confronted him with the fact that his wife had died of breast cancer, he replied, "Yes. But if I had made her go to the doctor sooner maybe she could have been saved. I killed her by not making her go to the doctor sooner."

- **Loss, emptiness, sadness, depression, loneliness**
  Of course, these emotions are the results of the loss of the person's physical presence in the mourner's life. Although they are natural and typical responses to loss, these emotions can be some of the most troublesome for mourners. Mourners often talk about being surrounded with people but feeling the most isolated and alone they have ever felt in their lives.

- **Relief and release**
  Mourners who experience a sense of relief or release at the death of a loved one often feel guilty or ashamed. The truth is that feeling relieved at the death of loved one who has been suffering is not a selfish, abnormal feeling. The relief comes in knowing loved one is no longer in pain or discomfort.
      Sometimes the person who died is loved, but they he or she made the lives of their loved ones stressful and even hellish. In these cases, the mourners may feel a sense of release in not having to endure the stressful relationship and life they shared with their loved one.

Mourners need to make self-care an important part of their grief. Here are some options for helping yourself to grieve in a healthy manner:

Practical Recommendations for Healing from the Emotional Trauma of Grief

- **Take time to heal.**
  Don't try to escape grief outbursts when they are happening. If you need to, retreat to a place (mentally or physically) where you can reflect on your feelings and your progress in grief without being distracted. Turn your cell phone off, and let the your voice mail screen your calls.

  Spend time privately writing your experiences and observations to allow yourself emotional release and understanding. A journal can serve later as a record of your grief walk and a reminder of how the journey has changed you.

- **Confide in someone who makes you feel safe and comforted.**
  Burdens shared with others are not as heavy. Accept the caring gestures and listening ears of others graciously. Recognize that your turn to listen and comfort someone else will come later. Don't be afraid to seek professional help when your grief and your life become overwhelming.

- **Ritualize the loss in a personally significant way.**
  Find creative ways to remember your loved one. Think of ways that honor the deceased, fit the person you are, and are a reminder of the transition you are undergoing. Holidays, birthdays, anniversaries and special days are often easier to endure when you plan to remember your loved one in a special way.

- **Allow yourself to change.**
Losses of people and the important roles they fulfilled in our lives change us. Don't resist that change. Try to see how you are changing, adapting to and maintaining your new relationship with your loved one. Embrace the changes in his or her honor. Find opportunities that exist for your emotional and spiritual growth, however bittersweet that growth may be.

- **Maintain a daily routine.**
This means take care of yourself physically, mentally, emotionally and spiritually. Consistency in your schedule and your self care becomes important in relieving stress in your grief. You may have no control over your life, but you can exercise some control over your activities.

  Get enough sleep – at least six to eight hours a night. On the days you can't sleep, at least rest. However, don't sleep too much. In the depression of grief, mourners can use sleep as an escape from the painful emotions of loss.

  Take cat naps whenever possible.

  Eat three meals a day. On days that food doesn't seem appealing, try to eat at least a little. At the same time, don't overeat and use food as a comfort measure. Watch your health and your weight.

  When physical problems occur, see your physician. Don't take for granted that your pain or discomfort may be totally related to stress or your grief. Mourners are more susceptible to real and very dangerous, life-threatening illnesses.

- **Exercise and stay active.**
  Exercise is a wonderful antidote for depression and the other draining emotions of grief. As we exercise, our bodies release endorphins. These proteins can help give us a feeling of well being, without the need for medications. If professionals suggest medications, take them under their supervision and only as prescribed.

- **Release anger.**
  Venting anger and other strong grief emotions can be done in either constructive or destructive ways. Remember, scripture admonishes us to "be angry and sin not" (Ephesians 4:26). Vent your anger in appropriate ways that will help you and not hurt you or others. Writing an angry letter <u>that you never intend to mail</u> and other creative measures can be used to cope with your anger in healthy ways.

  Please, remember to not mail the angry or emotional letter you write to vent your emotions. Sending the letter will only cause more problems. Also you might want to keep journals or diaries with private venting sessions in them under lock and key to prevent harm to others.

- **Pamper yourself.**
  There are several options for taking care of yourself in grief. Find ways to break a huge, impending task down into easy-to-achieve parts so it doesn't seem so overwhelming. Breathe deeply. Take walks. Watch sunsets and sunrises.

  Go out for dinner alone or with others. Sit and stare at the walls if that is all you have energy to do at that time. Ask for help from God and others, and don't feel guilty for asking.

- **Avoid chemicals.**
  Do not try to drown out the pain of loss and its emotions with alcohol or drugs. Self medicating is only a temporary relief. In some cases, alcohol and drug use or abuse can compound the problems of grief.

  Avoid stimulants such as caffeine, nicotine and sugar. These can add to the feelings of shakiness. People who consume caffeine in heavy amounts on a regular basis have a greater tendency to experience bouts of depression.

  Generally, medications are not needed. If they are, it should be for symptom relief so that you can function normally. **There are no magic pills for grief**. Treating yourself with prescription drugs or alcohol can be very dangerous. It's best to consult a physician before taking anything for the distress.

- **Be patient with yourself.**
  Healing takes time and energy. Mourners need to allow themselves time to grieve and to move toward healing. Resist the temptation to try to measure up to expectations that others have for us. All in all, the most important thing you as a mourner can learn to do is to exercise patience and gentleness with yourself.

- **Surround yourself with the beautiful and inspirational.**
  Music, art, poetry and other ways to reconnect with beauty and creativity can help lift the cloud

of despair that often hovers over us in grief. If you know someone who always makes you feel better when you are with them, keep their name and cell phone number nearby. Call them up occasionally for lunch and a good visit.

- **Cultivate an on-going sense of gratitude.**
  The burden of loss with its feelings of sadness, depression, anger, guilt and regret make it tough for mourners to remember the blessings in their lives—those people, things and situations for which we can still be thankful.

  One exercise that I give grief counseling clients is aimed at helping them to develop an attitude of gratitude. I tell the client to write a list of at least ten things for which they are thankful each night before they go to bed. The rest of the assignment calls upon the client to then pray the next morning to express thanks for each of the items on the list. By doing this exercise, the client ends each day in cultivating a sense of gratefulness and starts each day by expressing gratitude.

- **Use the resources available to you through your faith and spirituality.**
  Faith and religion can be great sources of comfort and strength for mourners. Faith resources include prayer, scripture reading and the support of your church family. Exercising your faith can provide consolation and help in finding reason and purpose in life in the middle of a crisis.

I'm caught in a maze and can't find my way out, blinded by tears of pain and frustration. I call to you, God; all day I call. I wring my hands, I plead for help.
(Psalms 88: 8-9 The Message)

CHAPTER TEN

LOVE AND GRIEF HAPPEN TO EVERYONE

The ability to experience loss is not restricted by your age, your understanding of life and death, your socio-economic status, your background, your belief system, your knowledge or your world-view. All of those factors making you a unique human being work together to shape how you choose to mourn or cope with your loss. Because love expressed as grief is universal, we can take heart as mourners that we are not alone. Other mourners of all ages and life situations are on similar grief journeys. Others, young and old, have experienced and endured comparable struggles in their grief. In their living grief well, we as mourners find hope that we can endure our challenges in grief also.

GriefWorks Commemoration 2007, Dallas, Texas.
(GriefWorks is a free children's grief support ministry of Christian-Works for Children)

It had been an emotional evening as children, teens, and adult family members gathered in early December to prepare for the difficult holiday season ahead. All of the GriefWorks children and their families had lost a significant loved one. Some of the children had lost a parent. Others had lost a sibling or a grand-

163

parent or an aunt or uncle. Although all of the losses in the children's grief support group were unique, all of the mourning families had one thing in common. They were all missing their loved one at a time of the year when the importance of family being together is stressed and so valued.

The most touching element of the annual GriefWorks Commemoration is a candle lighting ceremony in which children and family members can honor and remember what their missing loved one has given them. One by one the GriefWorks families came forward as their loved one's name was called. Each child lit a candle and had an opportunity to share some important, valued memory about their loved one.

Once the families had all lit a candle, we gave staff members and volunteers who had lost a loved one during the past year an opportunity to participate also. One by one the staff and GriefWorks volunteers lit candles and shared their losses with the group.

Just two months prior to the commemoration ceremony my 76 year-old mother had died of lung cancer. I struggled with the pros and cons of lighting a candle in tribute to her. Somehow at that time it seemed too soon for me to be able to share my very personal grief publicly. I wasn't sure if I could light the candle without having a major grief outburst in front of a group of impressionable, vulnerable children. (Yes, I know that grief outbursts are healthy but I, just like you, struggle at times with when and where it is appropriate for me to mourn publicly.)

But when the opportunity came, I lit the candle in honor of my mother. I shared with the group my mother's name, the details of her death and how much I would miss her. My tears welled up as I spoke, but the devastating grief outburst that I had feared did not happen.

After I closed the commemoration service with a prayer, one of our five year olds came up to me. She held out her arms and asked if I would give her a hug. The mother of this five year old had been brutally murdered. I never turn down a hug from a mourning five year old. As I leaned down to hug her, she whispered in my ear, "I know you miss <u>your</u> Mommy too."

I continue to be amazed that a five year old child can reach out from the depths of her sorrow over the loss of her young mother to comfort me, a man old enough to be her grandfather. We adults sometime wonder in our efforts to reach out to mourning children if they get our intended messages about grief. Believe me, children and teens in grief get it.

MISCONCEPTIONS ABOUT MOURNING CHILDREN AND TEENS

Our culture tends to view the grief experience of children in one of three ways. All three of these views lead to children and teens going through grief without the support and help that they desperately need.

First, children are often seen as incapable of understanding death at all. Therefore according to this view, children would never experience the emotions that come with a full understanding of death and loss. In other words, children cannot grieve.

This belief leads to mourning children being neglected, abandoned and feeling lost in their grief. Children and teens do experience love for the people in their lives. So it makes sense that the child's love will become grief when a loved one dies. Grief is another expression of love for bereaved people of all ages.

What children and teens need to help them cope with their potential misunderstandings or misconceptions of death and loss are the supportive, comforting role models of grieving adults in their lives. Young people in grief need someone to teach them about death and loss in terms that they will understand at their developmental stage.

Second, mourning children can be seen as "little adults" who can be comforted and counseled in the same way as adults in grief. This view can lead to the child having comforters who speak over their heads about death, loss and grief. In this view, the special needs of mourning children go unaddressed. When children in grief do not get the information they need and can understand, they make up fantasies and belief systems that can be harmful or destructive to their well being. When children are not given the support they need from adults, they devise unhealthy defense mechanisms that can become life-long destructive habits.

A good example of a bad coping skill developed by unsupported children in grief is the unhealthy coping skill of isolating from others and avoiding intimacy in relationships. It makes sense to the mourning child or teen that getting close to a loved one places them at risk of more possible loss and pain. These isolating children become adults who cannot achieve real intimacy in any relationship. This can lead to the mourning children having lives filled with failed marriages, relationships, friendships, careers and spiritual development.

Third, mourning children can be seen as more resilient than adults in grief. This belief leads to adults thinking that the child will soon get over the loss and move on. Children are resilient, but they are also fragile — emotionally, mentally, socially and spiritually. If the needs of a child or teen in grief are not addressed, the emotional wounds may not heal and secondary trauma can result in his or her life.

The greatest needs of a mourning child or teen are security and assurance that they are cared for. My son Christian taught this lesson to me one night when I came home from a social event at church. As I walked into the kitchen, I was confronted by my teenage son with his arms crossed and a frown on his face.

"You told us that you would be home at 10:30. It is now after 11:00. What happened?" asked Christian.

"Yeah, I'm sorry that I am late by a few minutes...." I replied.

"You are more than thirty minutes late!" Christian said cutting my apology short.

"Yeah....well, you see...the party ran a little longer than expected and I couldn't get away." I continued.

Christian leaned forward and asked slowly emphasizing each word, "And there were no phones so that you could call and tell us?"

My first thought at the moment was "Hey, now wait a minute! I have had this conversation before but you were the one who was late!" Then I suddenly understood what was happening. Christian had already suffered losses in his life, the losses of his mother and his baby sister. This time it was my failure to call ahead that caused him to realize that he might have to deal with another loss, the loss of his father.

Children are naturally egocentric. You need to understand that this doesn't mean children and teens are naturally and always selfish. Egocentricity in children is the result of their limited life experience, coping skills and mental development. Because of their restricted understanding and still-developing mental capacities, children think in very concrete rather than abstract term. This causes children to be unable to always separate themselves as individual human beings from their circumstances. Everything that happens in their lives is seen through the filter of how it affects them.

That is why children will ask such questions as "Now that mother is dead, who will make my lunch? Who will pick me up after school and take me to dance class? Who will tuck me in at night?" Frustrated mourning adults can often mistake these questions as a sign of the child being self-centered or selfish. The child wants assurances that he or she will be taken care of and that the danger of further catastrophic change in his or her life is over or limited.

Just weeks after the deaths of her mother and sister, my daughter Sarah hit me with a surprise question. "Dad, are you going to start dating now that Mom is gone?" The question of my social life and possible dating was not so much a surprise. I had already been told by my mother hours after the double funeral that she hoped that I would not live my life without a new spouse. Mother and other people in my life did not want me to be alone. Five weeks after the accident, a co-worker tried to set me up on a blind date with a church secretary that she knew I would enjoy meeting. Of course, early in my grief dating was the last thing on my mind.

What was surprising about Sarah's question was that I had never even considered that my children might be thinking about me entering the dating scene. But it is a logical question for bereaved children who have lost a parent. After I got over the initial shock of my daughter asking me about my personal life, I responded honestly, "Not any time soon. But if God brings a woman into our lives who I like and you could like, I guess that I could." Sarah seemed to be content with my answer.

A few months after that exchange, Sarah surprised me with another statement on my singleness and my social life. "Dad, I think that you are the type of man who once he loves and marries a woman like Mom that he could never fall in love or marry any other woman." Obviously Sarah was still thinking about what her life might be like if I started dating.

Then a few years later there was another surprising comment from my daughter about my potential dating life. "Dad, if you ever get remarried, will I have to call your wife 'Mother'?" Fortunately, her father heard Sarah's concern behind the obvious question. The real question Sarah was asking me was "How will your potential choices in your personal life affect me and my identity in this family?

I told Sarah, "If I do ever remarry, you will call my new wife by her first name. You won't have to call anyone else mother. No one can ever replace your mother."

Children are resilient, but they are fragile and deserve more care, comfort and support than the average adult mourner. They need to find security again in a world that is filled with the scary possibilities of more loss and change.

Children and teens will not quickly get over a major loss in their lives. Just like us adult mourners, they will need to accept and reconcile their new reality over their entire life. They will need to mourn the loss of their loved one on a regular basis. Young people revisit the losses and traumas of their childhood as they go through the developmental stages of their lives. They will need ongoing support and comfort for those times when they achieve great milestones in their lives. Each milestone is a reminder that their loved one is not with them physically to share the moment.

Helping Children Grieve

You can help mourning children and teens best by providing: 1) **security** to experience a safe environment to express grief and 2) **adult role models** who can teach them healthy ways to mourn the loss of their loved one. Here are some practical suggestions on how adults can help children in grief.

1. **Talk with your children about the death and their grief.**
   Do not be afraid to talk about death with children. Children are very intuitive. They realize their lives have changed and that things are not "all right" despite what some adults may tell them. Be honest concerning your feelings and your grief. You are teaching them how healthy adults deal with loss. Let your child know that it is healthy and safe to grieve, to talk about their thoughts and emotions and to remember their loved one on a regular basis.

2. **Model behaviors of grief for your child.**
   Children learn by mimicking the behavior of the adults around them. The important coping skills they learn from watching and following your example will prepare them for future losses and crises in their lives. When you are doing well in your grief, they will do well.
   I know personally how a parent or adult family member can affect a child's feeling of security and well-being. My mother and I shared a love for horror stories, on television and at the movies. We especially loved to watch any-

thing directed by the master of suspense Alfred Hitchcock.

Every Sunday night you could find my mother and me in front of the TV watching *Alfred Hitchcock Presents*. So you can understand how that when we found out that our favorite horror director had produced a new movie called *Psycho*, we were already making plans to get our theatre tickets.

Now if *Psycho* had come out today, nobody under 17 years of age would have been able to see it at the theatre. When *Psycho* came out it was 1961 and I was ten years old. There wasn't any movie rating system to prevent my mother from taking me to see *Psycho*.

In the darkened theatre watching *Psycho*, I had never been more frightened in my entire, short life. What was happening on the screen was not what was scaring me. What terrified me was my mother screaming, jumping and grabbing my arm in response to the movie. Here was my mother, my Rock of Gibraltar and the source of security for me, being scared out of her wits. I decided that if my mother was scared, this must be one scary movie.

How you as an adult react to grief affects how a child perceives the loss and chooses to respond to it. The coping skills you display in grief will mostly likely be the coping skills your child will adapt to get through this loss and future losses throughout his or her life.

3. **Let children decide if they attend the funeral or memorial.**
   If the child loves a person, they will mourn after that person's death. Let the child have a choice in participating in a funeral or memorial. Don't force them to stay away or go against their will. Explain to them before the ceremony what to expect when they are there. Answer their questions before, during and after the ceremony. Be honest and share information with the child in words that he or she can understand.

4. **Talk to your child's teachers and school counselors.**
   Make appointments to talk with the school staff about the loss and the concerns you have for your child. Set up a plan of action in case your child's grades or behavior change. Ask if the school counselor can meet with the child or be available if problems arise.

5. **Create a safe, secure environment for your child.**
   Maintain routines and schedules as much as possible. Show affection and assurance that the child is loved and will not be abandoned. If a parent has died, talk with the child about who will be taking care of him or her. Give lots of hugs and reassuring physical contact.
   An important part of creating a secure, loving environment for the mourning child or teen is to maintain consistent, fair rules and boundaries on what is appropriate or inappropriate conduct for the child at home, school and elsewhere. Parents and adults can give the mourning child

some leeway on behavior due to grief, but children need to know that the "rules" of acceptable behavior still apply to them. Grief can't be accepted as a good reason for acting badly.

6. **Let your child be free to feel and express grief emotions.**
Do not tell a child how they should feel or not feel about the loss. Encourage them to talk and listen patiently without judging or correcting them.

7. **Let your child be creative in coping with his or her grief.**
Give children an outlet to express their emotions. Make sure they have crayons, colored pencils and paper available if they enjoy art. Have them explain their creations. Do not censure or overreact to their expressions of grief.

8. **Create and use teachable moments with your child to talk about death.**
Find books that explain death and loss through stories for children and teens. Talk about the stories and answer their questions.

Other moments where you can talk about death and grief will sometimes just happen. When the child finds a lifeless insect or animal, explain death and being dead in terms the child can understand. When an insect or animal is dead, it can no longer breathe, eat, sleep or move. Make the comparisons of that observed death to when people die. You can also discuss how death affects the family of that person who died.

9. **Get help for your child and you when necessary**
Children are subject to complicated grief just like adults. But their symptoms are very different. If a child's behavior changes in significant ways, be sure to take them for help to specialists in dealing with children and grief.

10. **Use exact terms with your children when talking about death, dying and grief.**
Don't be afraid to use the words "death" or "die." Avoid using euphemisms such as passing away, going to sleep or losing the loved one.

Children don't understand these adult clichés about death, and they take what you say literally. When you say "We lost Grandpa," children will be wondering why you and the rest of the family are not sending out search parties to find him.

THE TRUTH ABOUT GRIEF AT ANY AGE

The comfort I received from a mourning five year old reminded me of two truths about grief. <u>First, love expressed as grief is universal.</u> The ability to experience loss is not restricted by your age, your understanding of life and death, your socio-economic status, your background, your belief system, your knowledge or your worldview. All of those factors making you a unique human being work together to shape how you choose to mourn or cope with your loss. No person who experiences love escapes loss and grief.

Because love expressed as grief is universal, we can take heart as mourners that we are not alone. Other mourners of all ages and life situations are on similar grief journeys. Others, young and old, have experienced and endured comparable struggles in their grief. In their living grief well, we as mourners find hope that we can endure our challenges in grief also.

Second, grief teaches and equips us for life — if we will just listen and come to terms with the lessons of loss. The messages sent to us in our own grief help us to be able to endure our grief and to comfort others. The lessons learned in our own grief also make it possible for us to educate those around us who have no clue how to minister to mourners.

These two truths about grief brought me to another insight—I have the resources and the responsibility to care for other mourners regardless of their age or situation. The five year old who ministered to me as I mourned the loss of my mother was compelled to do so by her personal grief experience and her benevolent heart. If a five year old mourner with limited understanding of death, coping skills and life experience can reach out to an adult mourner effectively, then any mourner can also feel compelled, equipped and competent to do the same for other mourners around him or her.

In reaching out in compassion to help other mourners, we all need to remember one important fact. We mourners are the experts on our own individual grief only. We are not the experts or directors of anyone else's grief. We can be the empathetic, supportive comforters for other mourners in our lives. As comforters of others, we let mourners we are with, take the lead in their own grief journey.

In our journey, the grief experience will shape us as individuals and will prepare us to be present for other mourners. If we just listen to the lessons of our own grief experience, we can become successful comforters for others.

Whether we reach out to others in their loss and sadness or coach comforters about our grief, both actions are choices available to us. I can guarantee you that God will place hurting people in your path who you will be equipped to help, support and encourage. I can also guarantee you that God will place people and opportunities in your life path to educate others in love about mourners, grief and loss.

Children and Teens in Grief

My successful five year old comforter at the GriefWorks commemoration has convinced me of the importance of making special efforts to support and comfort mourning children and teens. Children in grief are not too young or immature to feel the deep emotional trauma of loss and to suffer negative consequences. They may not understand death, loss or grief on an adult level, but they certainly feel the resulting pain of bereavement.

With limited coping skills and life experience, children and teens are especially vulnerable in grief. Too often adults make the mistake of neglecting young mourners and their needs. Too often adults are so overwhelmed by their own grief issues that they do not have the ability to see what the mourning children in their family are experiencing. Mourning adults have difficulties understanding what their own grief needs are—much less what their mourning children need.

Thank goodness there are children's grief support ministries like GriefWorks across the United States. And thank goodness that I, my son Christian and my daughter Sarah were able to attend a free children's grief support program, the Warm Place in Fort Worth, Texas. For almost a year and half at the Warm Place my children received the support and encouragement necessary to begin their individual grief journeys.

As a widowed single parent with two children, I was lost. I did not know what to do for myself or my children. When we found the children's grief support program in Fort Worth, it was exactly what we needed. Sarah and Christian were able to talk in a safe place with other mourning children near their ages. One of the things that my children enjoyed best about the grief groups was that everything said in the group stayed in the group. Everything shared was confidential.

One night as I was driving us home from the support groups, I tried to be the engaged, involved single father. I asked Christian and Sarah, "Well, how were your groups?" They rolled their eyes almost in unison and said, "Dad!! We can't tell you. The groups are confidential."

"I know," I said. "I don't want to know what was said. I was just wondering how the groups went."

In unison from the backseat of the car, Sarah and Christian repeated, "Dad!! The groups are confidential. We can't tell you." I understood. The children's grief support program with its confidential setting allowed my son and daughter to be totally honest about their grief experiences and their feelings...without having to worry what my reactions might be.

Thanks to caring, compassionate people who had experienced losses in their lives, my children and I received the necessary support and comfort to survive difficult times in our lives. I am convinced in my heart and soul that now it is my turn to share with other mourners the comfort that I and my children have experienced through God's messengers.

This past year I received a note from one of our widowed fathers in the GriefWorks support ministry:

"We are thankful for all your time and the work you have been doing with us. You have made a big difference in our grief journey.

"You know, before my wife died I was able to talk to her. I asked her that when she died and went to heaven to please send me and my son an angel to look over us and make us stronger. I think you through GriefWorks are that angel sent to help us during this difficult time. So thank you very much."

In the confusion and chaos of my early grief I had called out to God to send messengers who would help me to get through the dark times of my grief experiences. Now God is using me, the staff and volunteers at GriefWorks to send messages to children and their families to help during their difficult times in grief. God was helping me to navigate my grief journey and to keep my promise to pass along help and comfort to other mourners.

There are perks to allowing God to work through me and GriefWorks to help children and their families who are hurting because of the death of a loved one. First, I get to meet and help wonderful families at a time when they need support most. Second, I get to meet their wonderful loved ones through the stories and memories shared at GriefWorks. When anyone musters the courage to share with you the most intimate parts of their grief, you should feel complimented and blessed. You as a comforter have successfully made them feel safe to share the often hidden personal side of their lives.

Third, I learn more and more about grief and all its aspects with each mourning child, teen and adult who allows me to share time with them. God continues to take care of me and minister to me through these experts of grief.

God will place people in your life path to help. What will you do with what you have learned from your grief experience?

All praise to the God and Father of our Master, Jesus the Messiah! Father of all mercy! God of all healing counsel! He comes alongside us when we go through hard times, and before you know it, he brings us alongside someone else who is going through hard times so that we can be there for that person just as God was there for us. We have plenty of hard times that come from following the Messiah, but no more so than the good times of his healing comfort—we get a full measure of that, too. (2 Corinthians 1:3-5 The Message)

NOTE TO READER: In doing grief counseling and support groups, I am asked how my family, specifically my children are doing now. Without divulging extremely detailed personal information and possibly embarrassing my children, let me tell you how the Barber family is doing.

The number one question asked of me is "Have you remarried?" The answer is "No, not yet." Please don't get any ideas about blind dates or inviting me to a meal along with a surprise someone special. I have had that happen. It is embarrassing and awkward for me and the someone special. I am not opposed to dating or getting remarried, but I want to make those life-changing decisions on my own and without help.

The second most common question is how my children are doing today. My son and daughter are now all grown up and out on their own. They have turned out well and successful despite me. So far I am waiting for potential weddings and grandchildren.

Christian and Sarah grow more and more open about their thoughts and feelings as they see me more as an advisor and friend rather than a hovering, interfering father. We talk with fondness about our memories of their mother and their baby sister. Occasionally, but not often, we may talk about the accident itself. They both maintain to this day that they do not remember any of the details of that tragic day.

Sarah, who loves to write, sent me a potential children's book. It is the story of her grief experience as seen through the eyes of a young child...and in her words as a mourning daughter. Remember that as you read the following that this book and her story are copyrighted. You may share it with others, but please give my creative daughter, Sarah Barber, credit. Now read ahead and see for yourself how my daughter is doing in her grief.

Death is a Very, Very Long Time, But Not Forever

My name is Sarah and this is my family.

Something really bad happened to my family.

My family was in a car crash, and my mommy and my baby sister died.

Everyone says that they are up in heaven now with God.

Daddy says that death is a very, very long time, but not forever.

My family is very sad and we miss them very much.

Lots of people come and do things for our family, like bring us food.

My aunt even comes to stay with us for a while.

Lots of grown-ups say that they are sorry, but I don't know what for.

Lots of times I cry, because I miss them; and that's okay.

Sometimes I don't cry, and that's okay too.

Sometimes I feel like it's my fault.

Sometimes I'm mad at other people, like it's their fault.

Sometimes I wish my mommy and my sister were still with me, and sometimes I wish I was up in heaven with them.

I ask God why, because I don't understand why they're gone.

Daddy says nobody, but God knows why.

I go to a group with a lot of kids like me who are sad, because they miss someone who died.

The grown-ups there ask a lot of questions.

Sometimes I can talk about what happened, and that's okay

Sometimes my heart hurts too much to talk, and that's okay too.

Sometimes my friends ask me questions...sometimes people ask about my mommy, because they don't know...sometimes people ask if I have a sister...sometimes I don't know what to say to them.

Sometimes seeing other people's mommies and sisters makes me sad.

Sometimes it doesn't.

Sometimes I forget that they are gone, and it hurts when I remember.

Sometimes when I'm dreaming, I see my mommy and my sister, and I am so happy, but then my heart hurts when I wake up.

I will never stop missing my mommy and my sister, but I am starting to be less sad.

Death is a very, very long time, but not forever.

Love you lots,
    Sarah

CHAPTER ELEVEN

ALL THINGS ARE POSSIBLE

.... in order to survive the dark times of grief, the mourner must have hope and a belief that he or she will be given everything needed to travel the grief journey....in every grief the mourner questions and evaluates his or her belief system to some degree. Loss and grief force us to look at our faith and our spiritual beliefs to determine if they fit with the reality of life as it is being experienced. Questioning God or your faith during grief doesn't mean that you have lost your faith or your way. Grief tests our faith and can make it stronger.

May 17, 1993

In the waiting room at Baylor Medical Center, Dallas Texas.

"Oh, Larry! We lost her!" cried my sister-in-law Sally as her arms wrapped around me and pulled me into a forlorn and comforting squeeze. I had been grabbed suddenly from the stupor that had enveloped me and all the family members as we waited the news of my wife Cindy's second surgery following the accident. I went quickly from a stupor into numbness at the realization that I had just been told my wife of thirteen years had died. No! How could this be? My body went limp and I felt my knees collapse. I am sure that if Sally had not been hugging me tightly that I would have crumpled into a heap on the waiting room floor.

As Sally shared the horrific news with the rest of the family, I heard a spine-chilling wail from the other end of the waiting room. My sister Nancy and her family had arrived just at the moment we all learned that Cindy had died on the operating table. Nancy's over-powering, unnerving exclamation of sorrow combined with the mourning sounds of other family members caused my knees to buckle and I reached for the chair behind me.

As I sat down, sharp pains hit my chest and my breathing became fast and shallow. My brother Jason sat beside me and grabbed my arm. "My heart!", I whispered to Jason. "My heart is beating really fast, and I feel sick. Someone needs to check my heart."

I know that my reaction to Cindy's death threw a scare into the entire group of family members. I had been released earlier that day from Parkland Hospital. In the accident, the impact had thrown me against the car dashboard. Fortunately my seat belt had lessened the severity of the blow to my chest, but I did suffer a small puncture to one lung, and bruising to my heart. For the first few hours of my hospitalization, the staff had monitored closely my breathing and the erratic beating of my heart In the Parkland Hospital Emergency Room hooked up to a heart monitor, I had lived with the apprehension that I might be near death.

I had been advised to let anyone know if my heart ever felt "fluttery", a sign of arrhythmia which is an irregular heartbeat. To call my heartbeat fluttery at that moment of hearing that my wife had died would have been an understatement. I felt as if my heart was about to jump from my chest, I felt limp, and I was becoming dizzy. My body felt as much in chaos as my life had just become.

I felt myself being helped into a wheelchair and being pushed quickly down a hallway into a room with a heart monitor and a place for me to lie down. I had never felt so bad and helpless in my entire life. My life and my family were being demolished. How could I possibly survive all this? If I did, could I deal with life without my daughter Katie and my wife Cindy? Listening to the beep of a heart monitor, I was struck with the sudden horrifying fear that Christian and Sarah could become orphans.

At Parkland Hospital the staff attending to my care had thoroughly taught me about the heart monitor in my room there. They had told me that if my heart rate reached specific levels that I was to advise them. Today I couldn't tell you what that danger zone heart rate was, but in the Baylor Medical Center room those figures were fresh on my mind. I watched the heart monitor nervously as I realized that my heart rate was near the dangerous cardiac readings or entering into them. As I grew more anxious, I was finding it harder and harder to breathe. *"Oh, my Lord. Am I about to die of a heart attack? Oh, Lord, please no!"* I thought to myself and God.

Jason came into the room carrying his bible. I asked if he would read to me from Philippians 4. If I was about to die, I wanted to die listening to a favorite, comforting passage from God's Word and praying to Him. Jason began reading:

Rejoice in the Lord always. I will say it again: Rejoice!...I took another glance at the heart monitor as it edged up higher and more erratic. My breath felt more and more labored. I had never had an anxiety attack, but I was pretty sure that this was a genuine attack of some kind. Either that or I was dying. I closed my eyes and began to try to think of anything else.

Let your gentleness be evident to all. The Lord is near... I determined to not look at the heart monitor and took a deep breath trying hard to exhale slowly. I tried unsuccessfully to think of anything but the room I was in, the distress I was feeling and that stupid bleeping heart monitor. God, please help....

Do not be anxious about anything, but in everything, by prayer and petition, with thanksgiving, present your requests to God... I don't even remember consciously hearing the words Jason was reading from God's Word, but at some point I began to pray while breathing as slowly and deeply as my anxiety and sense of impending doom would let me. Dear Lord, be with us now. Bless my family. Bless Sarah. Bless Christian. Help this to pass quickly. Help me. Heal me. Let me feel your comfort and presence.

And the peace of God, which transcends all understanding, will guard your hearts and your minds in Christ Jesus... My apprehension wouldn't allow me to keep my eyes completely closed. I squinted and stole a glance at the heart monitor. My eyes opened wide. Was my heart rate slowing and becoming less wild?

I shut my eyes again; I tried to focus my thoughts and I returned to my prayer. *Please, Lord, let me feel your comforting presence. We need you now to be with us.....*

Finally, brothers, whatever is true, whatever is noble, whatever is right, whatever is pure, whatever is lovely, whatever is admirable—if anything is excellent or praiseworthy—think about such things... My breathing was becoming more relaxed. I stared again at the heart monitor. It was continuing to drop and becoming more stable.

Whatever you have learned or received or heard from me, or seen in me—put it into practice. And the God of peace will be with you. I looked from Jason to the monitor as he continued to read. Somehow I knew that we would be able to survive this moment. I was no longer thinking about the despair of leading my whole life without Katie and Cindy. I was thinking about how I could make it through this moment for Christian and Sarah. I would have to be content with my life as it was…with God's help.

…for I have learned to be content whatever the circumstances. I know what it is to be in need, and I know what it is to have plenty. I have learned the secret of being content in any and every situation, whether well fed or hungry, whether living in plenty or in want. I can do everything through him who gives me strength.

I am convinced that in order to survive the dark valleys of grief, the mourner must have hope and a belief that he or she will be given everything needed to travel the grief journey. In my grief I find my hope in believing that at the end of this life I will see Cindy and Katie in heaven. That hope that we are only temporarily separated is an important part of my belief system, my grief and my life.

Knowing I will see them again gives me the courage and energy to go on with life when my existence feels empty, senseless and hopeless in the threatening times of my grief. My faith helps me realize that there is always something important to wake up for and look forward to every day. And I can go on doing so as long as God keeps giving me days in which to wake up. I believe that God takes care of me, Christian and Sarah through the continuing crises of life so that we may one day be reunited as a family of five.

I am convinced also that in every grief the mourner questions and evaluates his or her belief system to some degree. Loss and grief force us to look at our faith and our spiritual beliefs to determine if they fit with the reality of life as it is being experienced. Questioning God or your faith during grief doesn't mean that you have lost your faith or your way. Grief tests our faith and can make it stronger.

Emily was a recent widow in one of my grief support groups. Her husband had been a minister for over thirty-five years. When he first developed cancer and went through chemotherapy, they had prayed along with everyone in their church and community that God would heal His minister.

Then the good news came from the oncologist to Emily and her husband. The cancer was in remission. The happy and thankful couple acknowledged God's healing hand through the treatments administered by the doctors. Instead of following their earlier plans to retire from the ministry, they pledged themselves to work even harder in leading the church and serving God.

Two years later the cancer returned with a vengeance. Three months after the second diagnosis, Emily's husband died, his body ravaged by the same type of cancer that they thanked the Lord for removing earlier in response to prayer. Two months after the death of her husband, Emily told our support group that she no longer believed in a loving, all-powerful God. In fact, she would tell the group about her disbelief in the Deity each time she retold her story.

Yet Emily at other times would talk about how she felt a struggle within her to hold onto hope despite her disappointment with God and how her life had changed. A fellow widow in the group put her arm around Emily and said, "I don't think that you have lost your belief in God or your faith. You talk about struggling. You are struggling with your belief in how God is supposed to work in your world. Therefore, you are struggling with God. And you can't struggle with God if you don't believe in Him anymore."

Perhaps you are questioning the beliefs you once held about how life is supposed to be and how you are to be treated in this world. Perhaps you are feeling that you are being punished for some unknown wrong you have done. Perhaps you are feeling helpless and hopeless spiritually. Remember that as long as you are struggling with these factors, you have not lost your belief, your faith or your hope. You are simply questioning what has happened to you and why. If you do determine your pre-grief beliefs to be illogical or unrealistic in your new reality of loss, now is the time to do deep soul-searching to find those beliefs and the faith that can give you hope again

Remember that you and your grief are not going to change overnight. Be patient with yourself as you search for meaning and purpose in your life after the death of a loved one. Grief is a process, not an event. You will find a new beginning and a new hope for the future to help you through your grief. It just takes time.

When Job heard this, he got up and tore his robe and shaved his head to show how sad he was. Then he bowed down to the ground to worship God. He said: "I was naked when I was born, and I will be naked when I die. The LORD gave these things to me, and he has taken them away. Praise the name of the LORD." (Job 1:20-21 NCV)

NOTE TO READER: What scriptures can I read to encourage me in my grief?

For my personal grief journey I find strength to endure loss and grief in comforting Bible passages which remind me of some important aspects of grief. Here are a few suggested Bible passages to study for potential insights into your grief.

- **PAUL'S ENCOURAGING WORDS TO GRIE-VING CHRISTIANS**
  (I Thessalonians 4:13-18)

The Apostle Paul shares encouraging words with Christians who have suffered the recent loss of cherished brothers and sisters in their church. The encouragement comes in the fact that God has promised to take care of His children whether they are alive or dead. All mourners— past mourners in the church in Thessalonica and mourners today—are given heart by hearing Paul's words that they will see their loved ones again when Jesus returns.

Paul explains to mourners that although they are not exempt from grieving over lost loved ones that:

1. The separation from their loved ones and the pain of grief caused by Death are only temporary and
2. There is hope even in the dark periods of grief. One day when Christ returns, mourners will be together again with their loved ones and with God and Jesus. Not only will this be a great homecoming for

believers, but it will be the greatest family reunion of all times.

The hope of our victory over Death in Jesus Christ and the promised family reunion in Heaven gives me the encouragement to face the struggles of grief and the crises of this life. I look forward to standing with the multitudes around God's heavenly throne, searching the crowd for familiar faces and staring once again into the eyes of my lovely wife Cindy and my beautiful daughter Katie.

This passage also alludes to the indestructibility of Love. God's love for us and the relationship He has with us is the same whether we are alive or dead. Our physical death does not end the love God continues to express for us. Our love for someone who dies is not ended at their death. Our loving relationship with that person continues. In their physical absence our continuing love finds voice in our grief and mourning.

- **JESUS WORKS A MIRACLE IN THE GRAVEYARD**
(John 11)

This is the story of the raising of Lazarus from the dead and of how Jesus Christ works miracles even in the graveyard where all hope appears to be gone. Jesus has been called to come to the aid of his friend Lazarus who has fallen ill. When he arrives he is confronted by Lazarus' grieving sisters Mary and Martha along with mourning family, friends and community members.

Twice in this passage we are told that Jesus is moved deeply. Despite the fact that Jesus is about to raise Lazarus from the dead to show God's power, He is emotionally devastated by the loss of His friend Lazarus and the grief being displayed by Mary, Martha and the others. In fact He is moved so deeply that He cries openly.

This scripture tells us that:

1. God is a God who cries with those that mourn. Jesus was the fullness of His Father in human form on earth. Jesus, His words and His actions represent God, His Words and His actions. Jesus the Son of God wept at the death of Lazarus and the grief of His dear friends. God cries with us as mourners following the deaths of our loved ones.
2. God and His Son Jesus can give us hope and encouragement in our sorrow. When Jesus saw Mary and Martha without hope in their grief, He gave them a reason to hope by saying, "I am the Resurrection and the Life…" Jesus gives us mourners that same hope today.

- **GOOD PEOPLE SUFFER**
  (Psalm 73)

This story of one man's suffering comes from the Hebrew poem authored by Asaph, the temple choir director. This message had a profound effect upon my wavering faith and my grief struggle.

Asaph suffers an unknown malady or crisis in his life that has become oppressive to him. This life crisis is causing Asaph to be consumed by his suffering day and night. His real struggle comes when he compares his life as a believer and servant of God to those of people whose word and actions mock God.

Asaph says that he has envied the wicked. He looked at them and saw that they prospered in the world and had everything that they wanted. Then he looked upon himself as one who served and trusted the Lord, only to suffer afflictions, trials and plagues. This was frustrating for Asaph. How could God make such a mistake? What good was it for Asaph to strive for purity when he received no benefit or reward from the God whom he served?

Then Asaph had an epiphany. Worshipping in the temple, listening to God's Word and being surrounded by God's people, Asaph's perspective of his situation changed. Only when his attitude and perspective changed, could Asaph realize that:

1. A merciful, caring God was always with him whether Asaph could or could not feel God's presence and comfort.
2. Good and bad things happen in this life to righteous and wicked people. The suffering caused in a person's life can blind him or her to the blessings of the moment from God. Humans can always look to others and think that those others have life much better than they do.
3. God will keep His promise to reward the good. Those who live in God's service will be rewarded.

4. God will keep His promise to reward the wicked. The evil and immoral of this world will eventually receive their punishment.
5. God is all that Asaph or any believer needs in this world or in Heaven.

Whom have I in heaven but you? And earth has nothing I desire besides you.

My flesh and my heart may fail, but God is the strength of my heart and my portion forever. (Psalm 73:25-26 NIV)

- **JOB'S STORY OF SUFFERING**
  (The Book of Job)

I don't think that it was a coincidence that after the accident and the funeral for my wife and daughter that I felt compelled to study the book of Job. The oldest book of the Bible, Job is a treatise on suffering and why man serves God. After I had finished my personal study of Job, a co-worker recommended a book for me to read. The book just happened to be an exposition of Job and the lessons to be learned in those scriptures about loss and suffering in this world.

Later in my studies for the ministry at the Center for Christian Education in Irving, Texas and through Abilene Christian University, I read the life-changing book *Yet Will I Trust Him: Understanding God in a Suffering World* by Dr. John Mark Hicks. (Hicks, College Press Publishing, 1999). The title is a quote from Job stating that even if God takes his life, he will still put his full faith in God.

Dr. Hicks writes of the role of suffering from his theological education and his life experience of losing his first wife to a post-surgical blood clot and later his teenage son to a debilitating disease. I recommend this book to all ministers, chaplains, lay counselors and Christian grief counselors.

What can Job teach us mourners?

1. Those who believe and serve God are not exempt from experiencing losses and suffering in life.
2. God is more interested in us being faithful than in our being comfortable in this life.
3. As sufferers, we do not have the big picture or understanding why events happen the way they do in our lives. Even when we may search for answers to why life is the way it is, we may never get the answers.
4. God cares for His children and will reward them.
5. God is on His throne and in control. This can be the source of great comfort or sometimes great frustration for those who serve God.
6. Comforters should not choose to speak for God on why someone suffers. (Just ask Job's friends – Eliphaz, Bildad, and Zophar and the young spokesman Elihu.)

In addition to these passages, mourners might want to keep the following list of Bible verses handy when difficult emotions arise in their grief.

COMMON GRIEF FEELINGS & BIBLE-CENTE-RED GRIEF SUPPORT

- **"IT'S IMPOSSIBLE!"**
  All things are possible – Luke 18:27

- **"IT'S HOPELESS!"**
  In Christ, you grieve with hope – I Thessalonians 4:13-18

- **"I'M TOO TIRED!"**
  I will give you rest – Matthew 11:28-30

- **"I CANNOT GO ON!"**
  My grace is sufficient – II Corinthians 12:9 & Psalms 91:15"

- **"I CANNOT DO IT!"**
  You can do all things – Philippians 4:13

- **"I CANNOT FIGURE IT OUT!"**
  I will direct your steps – Proverbs 3:5-6

- **"IT'S NOT WORTH IT!"**
  It will soon be worth it all – Romans 8:28f

- **"I CANNOT FORGIVE MYSELF!"**
  I forgive you – I John 1:9 & Romans 8:1

- **"I CANNOT MANAGE!"**
  I will supply all your needs – Philippians 4:19

- **"I AM AFRAID!"**
  I have not given you a spirit of fear – II Timothy 1:7

- **"I AM ALWAYS WORRIED & FRUSTRATED!"**
  Cast all your care on Him – I Peter 5:7

- **"I DO NOT HAVE ENOUGH FAITH!"**
  I've given everyone a measure of faith – Romans 12:3

- **"I AM NOT SMART ENOUGH!"**
  I give you wisdom – I Corinthians 1:30 & James 1:5

- **"I FEEL ALL ALONE!"**
  I will never leave you or forsake you – Hebrews 13:5

CHAPTER TWELVE

YOU ARE MORE THAN YOUR GRIEF

...love never dies and deaths do not kill relationships. Grief is just another expression of the love that you have for the person who died. Love in the form of grief makes you miss the person, hurt for the loss, and honor your loved one with your life. The best monument or memorial you can build to your loved one's memory is to live a good life, mourn in a healthy way and reach out to help other mourners.

Rose Hill Cemetery, Cleburne Texas, August 1979.

I cannot imagine what Cindy must have thought sitting across from her exuberant fiancé in the front seat of my white 1976 Ford Futura (with cardinal red interior!) Without an explanation I had driven her to the city cemetery. Cindy and I were in Cleburne just a half hour drive south of Fort Worth. We had travelled from the Texas Panhandle so that Cindy could meet my family shortly after she had accepted my marriage proposal. Now she was probably regretting having said yes.

We had known each other for three weeks. But I was deeply, madly, truly in love with this petite 23 year old vibrant blonde whom I had met backstage at the community theatre in Amarillo, Texas. We were both in separate acts of the Amarillo Little Theatre's production of *Plaza Suite*, a Neil Simon play. All three acts of the play take place in the same room of the famous New York hotel. I played the Hollywood playboy writer in one act and Cindy was the reluctant bride hiding in the bathroom before her wedding in another act. Cindy must have really felt like the reluctant bride to be as we drove up and down the roads of what was to her an unfamiliar cemetery. How romantic.

"Here we are," I said, parking the car. I jumped out of the front seat, ran to open Cindy's door and took her hand. (No, it was not the only or last time that I ever opened the car door for her!) "I want you to meet some more family members."

With that being the only explanation of our trip to the local graveyard, I escorted Cindy toward two monuments. "This is my grandmother Sarah Elizabeth Barker. She died shortly after I was born. I never really got to know her."

"Oh, your mother's mother! So your mother's maiden name is Barker?" asked Cindy laughing slightly. "And her married name is Barber."

"Yes, my mother's legal name is Betty Barker Barber," I said. Cindy, whose bizarre sense of humor had attracted me to her, chuckled. It took me a second to get why she was laughing. "Yeah, Betty Barker Barber!"

"Well, she didn't have to change her monogrammed towels, I guess," replied Cindy.

"And this is my sister Karen," I said smiling and pointing to a smaller headstone with a lamb engraved above my baby sister's name.

I felt compelled to bring Cindy to the Rose Hill cemetery because it had been a major part of my childhood. I wanted to share this part of my life with her. At least once a month, my mother had visited the gravesites bringing me and my siblings with her. I didn't know it at the time, but my mother spoke with her mother during each visit and kept her updated on our family developments. I think too that Mother had wanted her children to know their grandmother and sister personally and how important they were.

I never knew how much death and loss had shaped my childhood and me as a person until I lost Cindy and Katie. Some fourteen years later Cindy would revisit the Rose Hill Cemetery. There she and Katie would be lowered into the ground at the end of a solemn graveside ritual. The ritual was in sharp contrast to the double funeral with over 400 friends and family members in attendance at the church. I remember that the reality of their deaths did not strike me until the moment I saw their caskets going slowly into the graves.

Losing a grandmother had been a huge factor in shaping my experiences as a child. Since my father's parents lived so far away, we rarely saw them. My mother's father went off to live with an uncle whom we never saw. So I grew up feeling cheated of having grandparents nearby to spoil me like my friends were spoiled by their grandparents. Death had made me different than all the other children. They had grandparents active in their lives. I did not. As a child, I thought that I was either the victim of a cruel, unfair fate or that I was being punished for being less than I should be.

Now as a grown-up I know better. I wasn't being punished for being a bad child. I had lost a grandmother and sister for one reason. Death happens... to good and bad people...and in every family. The absence of my grandmother physically with us had nothing to do with what kind of child I was, what I said or what I did. The death of my grandmother and baby sister were just sad facts of life. The same situation could and does happen to other people and other families.

The same statement can be said about the deaths of my wife Cindy and my daughter Katie. Their deaths happened independently of what kind of man I am, what I believe, what I say or what I do. Their deaths do not define me. Their deaths do not change what kind of man I am, chose to be, or my identity.

Their deaths are sad, tragic facts of life. Also their deaths do not define them either. How, when or where they died does not define them as people, their talents or their character.

Certainly what defines Cindy and Katie is how they lived their lives and influenced other people for the short time they were here. Their lives speak more eloquently about them as people than I ever could. My children and I will be defined not by our losses but by how we choose to live and influence others.

The same statements can be made about your loved ones, their deaths and you. You and your loved ones are not defined by the loss or how they died. Your loved ones are defined by how they lived. You are defined by how you choose to live after the tragic losses in your life.

My mother never "let go" of her mother and baby daughter. She shared with me that many had told her as a young grieving woman in her twenties to let go and get over the losses. But she could not. She knew instinctively that her grief advisors were wrong in what they prescribed for her.

She remembered her mother and baby, loved them, and carried them into her future with her and her family.

She made sure her mother's grandchildren and her baby daughter's siblings knew who Sarah Elizabeth Barker and Karen Barber were. My mother made them an important part of our childhood and our memories to carry with us into the future. Her suppression and avoidance of dealing with difficult and painful grief emotions is what consumed her life eventually and caused her to implode emotionally though. Remembering my mother did well. Mourning in a healthy way she didn't.

In hindsight I can now see that my mother taught me and my family that love never dies and deaths do not kill relationships. Grief is just another expression of the love that you have for the person. Love in the form of grief makes you miss the person, hurt for the loss, and honor your loved one by how you choose to live after the death. The best monument or memorial you can build to your loved one's memory is to live a good life, mourn in a healthy way and reach out to help and support other mourners.

Although I may not have the privilege of meeting you personally, I can say honestly and sincerely that I am saddened by your loss. The death of your loved one is truly a loss to you, your family, your community and all of mankind. Each life is precious and has purpose. I congratulate you on your struggle through grief to this point. I also congratulate you on making the decision to educate and arm yourself for the future part of your grief. You have made a healthy, wise decision. No one is meant to go through grief alone and without help.

Both you and I have been victims of death, loss and grief. We had no choice in that. But we do have the choice on how we respond to our grief and to life. I pray that your choices are the wisest and most healthy possible. Don't be afraid or reluctant to ask for help along the way. Remember that how you choose to live will determine your health and your emotional and spiritual well being.

You do not have to detach or let go of the person who died. Determine to take your loved one with you always by living a good life, mourning in a healthy way and treasuring your memories. Don't avoid grief because the unique grief you experience is the continued love you will always express toward your special loved one.

I will turn their mourning into gladness. I will give them comfort and joy instead of sorrow. (Jeremiah 31:13 NIV)

A GRIEF WELL LIVED

You may not have the same background or beliefs that I do. I am convinced though that you or any mourner has the potential to find the hope and the promise to be fully equipped for a healthy, meaningful grief journey. Grief is never easy, but grief becomes easier with hope, information and a good support system of friends, family and loved ones. Unashamedly I share with you that I found all of these resources through my best friend God and His family the church

The chapel of the South MacArthur Church of Christ, Irving Texas.

I was getting more and more nervous as the church members filed into the chapel for a special message this Wednesday night. You see, I was going to present that evening's message on grief and loss. The church minister Grady King knew me and my grief history. His church had gone through a season of loss with the deaths of several church family members.

"Larry, do you do presentations on grief?" Grady had asked me just a few weeks earlier.

"No…uh…I've lead some grief support groups, but no presentations…yet. Uh…no, I haven't," I mumbled as my heart sped up with the thought of speaking to a group larger than my usual grief group of three to five participants.

"Would you be willing to do a three part Wednesday night series for South Mac?" asked Grady. "We've had several deaths recently and I know that you would be able to share something that our church members need to hear." Grady explained that plans had already been made to start a grief support group open to church members and the community following my three-part grief series. That is, if I agreed to do the series.

"What? Me? Present a three-week series to a whole church?" I thought to myself as Grady continued. *"I don't know if I have enough information to fill up three whole Wednesday night services. And who am I to tell other hurting people how to deal with their grief and lead their lives?"*

Grady paused. A broad, encouraging smile came across his face. I wondered if he had suddenly been able to read my thoughts of fear and self-doubt. "If you need time to think about it, I understand," said Grady. "I really believe that what you could share with the church would be helpful."

"Oh, I don't need to think about it. I am honored that you asked," I said.

Larry! What are you saying? Maybe you had better think it over. I don't know if you are ready," said my self-doubt. *"You can't do this without some additional help or study or time or something!"*

"Sure, I would be glad to do the series," I stammered finding the courage to accept Grady's offer. "What nights?"

The self-doubt had continued for the weeks leading up to the Wednesday night church series. What had I gotten myself into? What would happen if I said something wrong and messed up someone's life horribly? As I sat on the pew waiting to be introduced, my inner struggle persisted.

Grady stepped up to the front of the chapel. I began to pray that God would give me His healing words to speak that night. I prayed that what He gave me to say would comfort and support the hurting. I prayed that all that happened in the chapel tonight would honor God and how He had helped me and my children. I prayed that what I said would cause nobody to get hurt. Please don't let me embarrass you, God.

As Grady shared with the group my story of loss, I could feel the atmosphere in the room change. Suddenly an empowering feeling of acceptance enveloped me. But that was only the beginning. Then something unexpected happened.

Grady asked me to step forward. He asked the elders of the church to stand around me. As the group of church leaders began to pray, they laid their hands upon me.

"Dear Father. Be with Larry tonight as he shares his story and your words of comfort for the grieving. Give him the courage to speak to the hearts of the hurting here. Touch the hearts of the grieving here tonight... which includes all of us. Let them be open to what you have given Larry to share.

"Bless Larry and his ministry to mourners here and elsewhere. Help his ministry to grow and your name to be glorified. In Jesus' name we pray. Amen."

I had never in my entire life had anyone lay their hands on me and pray for me. That moment in the South MacArthur chapel has to be one of the most personally moving and inspirational moments of my life as a Christian. I am tearing up now as I write this wondering if Grady and the elders knew what their prayer was stirring within me—a need to tell others my grief experiences. That compulsion continues today.

Remember that I said that God has the ability to give you everything that you need to keep your promises to Him. I had promised to share with other mourners whatever God would share with me through His messengers. I am convinced beyond a shadow of a doubt that the moments I prayed for divine help at the scene of the May 1993 accident and weeks later in the counselor's office, God had already set in motion the events, people, and insights that would equip me to not only support and comfort me and my family, but to help others.

Since my grief journey began I do not believe in coincidences in life. You can try to convince me to see that all that has happened to me and my children is just a random series of events leading me to where I am today. Like Joseph talking to his brothers (Genesis 50:19-20) I credit God for turning everything that was meant for harm in my life into events that work toward good. In every detail of our grief journey, God has been working in the background. He has answered my prayers to be present in the lives of me, my son and my daughter. Here is my evidence:

- As I prayed inside the wreckage of the accident for Jesus' presence and God's help, my seriously injured wife had enough thought to share with emergency medical technicians and the investigating police officers the names and phone numbers of her family and my family. She also shared with them contacts at the Richland Hills Church of Christ in Fort Worth and our Bible school class -the New Directions Class.

As a result, within hours of our going to three different hospitals, family members and church family stood vigil in waiting rooms as Sarah, Christian, Cindy and I went through medical evaluation and treatment. I believe God was making His presence known through His people and their prayers for us.

- Days after the accident, two couples in our small study group at church mailed out letters soliciting prayers and support for our family to churches around the community. I still have the hundreds of sympathy cards, notes and personal support responses from fellow believers we knew and did not know.
- Over four hundred family members, friends, church members and people from the community attended the funeral service for Cindy and Katie on May 19, 1993.
- The chaplain at Cooks Children Medical Center in Fort Worth brought the founder and director of the Warm Place, Peggy Boehme, to Sarah's hospital room. There Peggy, who had lost her son, told us about their support services for grieving children and their families. She said that they had already reserved places for me, Christian and Sarah in their groups. We attended those grief support groups for nearly a year and a half.
- Scores of people showed their support and love by providing food, cleaning our home, mowing our lawn, and countless phone calls and visits to see how we were doing.
- I had a personal visit with the man who had resuscitated Sarah at the scene of the accident. He shared that he had been so personally moved by the incident and our responses of faith in crisis

that he had decided to return to church. He was going to give God another chance to change his life.

- Due to the support of individuals in our Bible school class and the Richland Hills church of Christ along with family and friends, I was able to pursue my Masters Degree in Biblical Studies from Abilene Christian University through their off-campus program at the Center for Christian Education in Irving, Texas. I was the first person to complete the new off-campus Masters Degree in Biblical Studies program.
- I volunteered to work with the Grief Recovery Ministry of Richland Hills Church of Christ in Fort Worth. There I was mentored with love and guidance as a new grief group facilitator.
- I started attending meetings of HOPE (Helping Other Parents Endure) a weekly bereaved parent support group. After a few sessions the director and founder of HOPE, Donelle Herron asked me to co-facilitate the group with her. I facilitated HOPE groups for almost four years.
- After I accepted Grady King's invitation to teach about grief at South MacArthur Church of Christ, other churches began to extend me the same invitation.
- In 2000 one of the Center for Christian Education board members, Cullen Johnson, invited me to Dallas for a tour of a new children's grief support program called GriefWorks. I was hoping desperately that he would offer me a position at GriefWorks. But I wasn't supposed to work there…yet.
- Only weeks after my graduation from the Center for Christian Education, the director Ronnie

Wiggins offered me a job helping the staff who trained ministerial students for service. Under Ronnie's and the staff's encouragement, I continued my studies of scripture and grief and loss. It was during this time that I was able to receive support and encouragement from the writings and teachings of Dr. John Mark Hicks of Lipscomb University in Nashville, Tennessee and Dr. Virgil Fry of Life Line Chaplaincy of Houston, Texas.

- The funds became available for me to work on a Masters Degree in Counseling from Amberton University in Garland, Texas. My interest in grief counseling became strong after my first course there, *Psychological Perspectives of Death and Dying,* taught by Dr. John Scott who works now for Christian Care Centers in Mesquite, Texas. John's interest in death and grief stemmed from the loss of his father as a young child. He had facilitated grief support groups at the Warm Place in Fort Worth and GriefWorks in Dallas.

- After my graduation with my counseling degree, I gave notice that I was leaving the Center for Christian Education to pursue a yet-to-be-found opportunity where I could practice grief counseling. Just two weeks before I was scheduled to leave the Center, I was offered the job as the first full-time bereavement coordinator with Odyssey HealthCare, a hospice in Fort Worth. For the next six years I maintained the bereavement counseling and support for a case load of several hundred families a year.

- My new employer made it possible for me to have funds and the time off to begin studies at the internationally recognized Center for Loss and Life Transition in Fort Collins, Colorado under the supervision of Dr. Alan D. Wolfelt. It has been my blessing to be able to go to the Center for Loss six times for bereavement support training in seven years.

Dr. Wolfelt had started the Center for Loss and Life Transition because of his history of loss. After the death of a close friend at the age of sixteen he penned a mission statement to create a place where mourners could receive comfort and education to help them and others through grief.

- My hospice job also made it possible for me to be certified in Thanatology (the specialized study of death, dying and bereavement) through the Association of Death Education and Counseling.
- While working in Fort Worth, I became acquainted with Jamie Jewell, the community relations director for the funeral homes of Dignity Memorial. Jamie hired me to do evening time grief support groups in Dignity Memorial facilities in Fort Worth and Arlington.
- In April 2007, I came to work for ChristianWorks for Children. I currently direct the GriefWorks ministry which provides children and teens ages 5-18 and their family members free grief support. GriefWorks touches the lives of over thirty grieving families per month. GriefWorks allows me to do community grief support groups for adults, community grief support presentations and grief support seminars for professionals.

I believe that it is no coincidence that my employer ChristianWorks for Children is the ministry which helped my wife Cindy and me adopt our daughter Katie. I feel I have come full circle in coming to work for this ministry dedicated to helping children and their families.

I have asked for God's presence, His help and His guidance in my life. I believe that He has answered my prayers and more.

With God's power working in us, God can do much, much more than anything we can ask or imagine. (Ephesians 3:20 NCV)

Remember that I told you that I have discovered that mourners need to find a reason to hope and to feel the promise that they will have what they need to make it successfully through their grief journey? You may not have the same background or beliefs that I do. I am convinced though that you or any mourner has the potential to find the hope and the promise to be fully equipped for a healthy, meaningful grief journey. Grief is never easy, but grief becomes easier with hope, information and a good support system of friends, family and loved ones. Unashamedly I share with you that I found all of these resources through my best friend God and His family the church.

My wish for you is that you allow the events of your life, good and bad, to guide you in your grief journey toward healing, hope, peace and joy. Don't be afraid to ask for help. Be open and listen to the healing messages and comforting messengers that come into your life and your grief. Pray without ceasing for guidance. God will answer your prayers for help, support and consolation. And then, one day...God will send **you** to be the messenger of hope and the answer to the prayers of other mourners.

"The Spirit of the Lord God is upon me, because the Lord has anointed me to bring good news to the afflicted; He has sent me to bind up the broken-hearted... to comfort all who mourn, to grant those who mourn in Zion, giving them a garland instead of ashes, the oil of gladness instead of mourning, the mantle of praise instead of a spirit of fainting."
Isaiah 61:1-3 NIV

CPSIA information can be obtained at www.ICGtesting.com
Printed in the USA
240230LV00003B/1/P